Student Research Workshop 2017

Associated with the 11th International Conference on Recent Advances in Natural Language Processing (RANLP 2017)

Varna, Bulgaria
4 - 6 September 2017

ISBN: 978-1-5108-5523-6

Printed from e-media with permission by:

Curran Associates, Inc.
57 Morehouse Lane
Red Hook, NY 12571

CURRAN ASSOCIATES INC. proceedings.com

Some format issues inherent in the e-media version may also appear in this print version.

Printed by Curran Associates, Inc. (2018)

Association for Computational Linguistics
209 N. Eighth Street
Stroudsburg, Pennsylvania 18360

Phone: 1-570-476-8006
Fax: 1-570-476-0860

acl@aclweb.org

Additional copies of this publication are available from:

Curran Associates, Inc.
57 Morehouse Lane
Red Hook, NY 12571 USA
Phone: 845-758-0400
Fax: 845-758-2633
Email: curran@proceedings.com
Web: www.proceedings.com

TABLE OF CONTENTS

Dish Classification using Knowledge based Dietary Conflict Detection

Nadia Clairet
LIRMM (Laboratoire d'Informatique, de Robotique et de Microélectronique de Montpellier)
860 rue de St Priest 34000 Montpellier, France
LIMICS (Laboratoire d'Informatique Mdicale et d'Ingnieurie des Connaissances en e-Sant)
74 rue Marcel Cachin 93017 Bobigny, France
Lingua et Machina
7 Boulevard Anatole France, 92100 Boulogne-Billancourt, France
clairet@lirmm.fr

Abstract

The present paper considers the problem of dietary conflict detection from dish titles. The proposed method explores the semantics associated with the dish title in order to discover a certain or possible incompatibility of a particular dish with a particular diet. Dish titles are parts of the elusive and metaphoric gastronomy language, their processing can be viewed as a combination of short text and domain-specific texts analysis. We build our algorithm on the basis of a common knowledge lexical semantic network and show how such network can be used for domain specific short text processing.

1 Introduction

The dish classification according to some dietary criteria is a challenging task. Performing such classification given the dish title as it may appear in a restaurant menu implies solving the following issues: context scarcity, relevant information selection, and output qualification. In the framework of our method, these issues have been dealt with following two steps. First, domain specific knowledge[1] has been immersed into a large general knowledge lexical semantic network. Second, a graph traversal algorithm has been defined and parametrized in order to grasp relevant lexical and semantic information for the dietary conflict detection.

In terms of structure, the network we use is a directed graph where nodes may represent simple or compound terms, linguistic information, phrasal expressions, and sense refinements[2]. The arcs of the graph are directed, weighted, and typed according to the ontological, semantic, lexical associations between the nodes. They also may be semantically annotated (ex.: *quiche* $\xrightarrow[frequent]{part-whole}$ *egg*) which is convenient for working with domain specific expert knowledge. During the traversal (interpretation) of the graph, the nodes and the arcs are referred to as respectively *terms* and *relationships.*. Throughout this paper, *relationship* corresponds to a quadruplet $R = \{term_{source}, type, weight, term_{target}\}$. *Weight* denotes an association force of the relationship between two terms of the graph.

The paper will be structured as follows. First, we will recall main state-of-the-art achievements related to short text analysis and cooking recipe analysis. Second, we will detail materials of the approach: knowledge resource structure, text preprocessing steps. Third, we will describe our graph traversal method. Finally, we will present and discuss the output of our system and introduce its possible evolutions.

2 State of the Art

2.1 Distributional Methods for Short Text Analysis

The processing of dish titles can be considered as a possible specialization of some general method for short text analysis. Given the importance of the distributional hypothesis[3] in the current NLP practice, we will empathize knowledge based distributional method and logic based distributional method to the short text processing. A relevant knowledge based distributional method has been proposed by (Hua et al., 2015) in the framework of the Probase[4] lexical semantic network. The

[1] Terms and relationships related to nutrition, cooking techniques, cooking recipes and their typical parts, diets and typical dietary restrictions.

[2] Unlike the dictionary sense, the sense refinement reflects the typical use of a term, its sense activated by a particular context.

[3] The main idea behind the distributional hypothesis : "a word is characterized by the company it keeps"(Firth, 1957).

[4] https://www.microsoft.com/en-us/research/project/probase/.

Proceedings of the Student Research Workshop associated with RANLP 2017, pages 1–9,
Varna, Bulgaria, 4-6 September 2017.
http://doi.org/10.26615/issn.1314-9156.2017_001

Probase associated tools allow obtaining a concept distribution based on different scoring functions (conditional probability distribution[5], point-wise mutual information[6] etc.). Prior to the analysis of short texts, the authors in (Hua et al., 2015) acquire knowledge from web corpus, Probase network as well as a verb and adjective dictionary. They solve the segmentation task by introducing a multi-fold heuristic for simple and multi-word term detection. It takes into account the presence of *is-a* and *co-occurrence* relationships between the candidate terms. Subsequently, the terms are typed according to different categories : part of speech, concept/entity distinction etc. Finally, the disambiguation is done using the weighted vote (conceptual connections of the candidate term considering the "vote of context"). This method seems to be relevant for queries, however it would be difficult to use it for the dish classification. The main difficulty comes from the fact that it is concept driven. Indeed, for a term such as "creme brulee", we obtain the concept distribution scores shown in Table 1. Due to the underlying semantic relationship types (*is-a,relatedness*), these examples bring very few information about the composition and the semantic environment (that needs considering relationship types expressing *part-whole, location, instrument, sensory characteristic* relationships) of the dish titles and one can hardly qualify some of the returned scores (e.g. *off beat flavor*) in order to approximate the underlying relationship type. An improvement of the knowledge based distributional method could be made using an additional semantic resource containing a rich part-whole semantics[7] such as WordNet (Fellbaum, 1998).

Term (concept)	MI	$P(concept\|entity)$
dessert	0.386	0.446
authentic bistro dish	0.164	0.12
off beat flavor	0.047	0.06
homemade dessert	0.046	0.048
dairy based dessert	0.04	0.036

Table 1: Concept distribution for *creme brulee* (Probase conceptualization tool)

A different kind of methods for short text analysis relies on general-purpose first order probabilistic logic as shows the hybrid approach developed by (Beltagy et al., 2014). The authors use them to generate an on-the-fly ontology that contains the relevant information related to some current semantic analysis task. They adopt probabilistic logic as it allows weighted first order logic formulas. The weight of the formulas corresponds to a certainty measure estimated from the distributional semantics (meaning representation, semantic relation prediction). First, natural language sentences are mapped to a logical form (using the Boxer tool (Bos, 2015)[8]). Second, the ontology is encoded in the form of weighted inference rules describing the semantic relations (the authors mention *hyponymy, synonymy, antonymy, contextonymy* i.e. the relation between "hospital" and "doctor"). Third, a probabilistic logic program answering the target task is created. Such program contains the evidence set, the rule base (RB, weighted first order logical expressions), and a query. It calculates the conditional probability $P(Query|Evidence, RB)$. This approach has been tested on the SICK[9] data for the tasks of semantic textual similarity detection and textual entailment recognizing. The results showed a good performance of this method over distributional only and logic only methods. This kind of approaches rather considers lexical relations (revealing some linguistic phenomena), than purely semantic (language independent, world knowledge phenomena) relations. As the knowledge based distributional method, it suffers from the difficulty to qualify the relationships as it uses mainly the co-occurrence analysis.

[5]Conditional probability distribution of two discrete variables (words)

$$P(A|B) = \frac{P(A) \cap (B)}{P(B)}$$

[6]Point-wise Mutual Information is calculated according to the formula :

$$PMI(x; y) = \log \frac{P(x, y)}{P(x)P(y)}$$

[7]The WordNet part-whole relation splits into three more specific relationships : *member-of, stuff-of,* and *part-of.*

[8]Boxer (Bos, 2015) is a semantic parser for English texts based on Discourse Representation Theory.

[9]*Sentences Involving Compositional Knowledge.* This dataset includes a large number of manually annotated sentence pairs that are rich in the lexical, syntactic and semantic phenomena (e.g., contextual synonymy, syntactic alternations). `http://clic.cimec.unitn.it/composes/sick.html`.

2.2 Cooking Instruction Analysis

Besides the approaches focused on flavor networks which consider cooking recipes as "bags of ingredients" such as (Ahn et al., 2011), the existing approaches to the recipe analysis concentrate on recipes taken as a sequence of instructions that can be mapped to a series of actions. Numerous publications concern the implementation of supervised learning methods. For instance, (Mori et al., 2012) use the annotated data to extract predicate-argument structures from cooking instructions in Japanese in order to represent the recipe as a work flow. The first steps of this process are words segmentation and entity type recognition based on the following entity types: Food, Quantity, Tool, Duration, State, chefs action, and foods action. Therefore, this task is similar to the conceptualization process proposed by (Hua et al., 2015) discussed in the previous section. Entity type recognition is followed by syntactic analysis that outputs a dependency tree. The final step aims at extracting predicate-argument triples from the disambiguated (through segmentation, entity type recognition, and dependency parsing) recipe text. In this approach, the semantic information that could be attached to the arcs is attached to the nodes. The node type together with the syntactic markers (i.e. case marker) helps determining the nature of the predicate-argument relation. This method yields modest results and could be improved by adopting a more versatile graph structure (i.e. a structure with typed arcs). (Kiddon et al., 2015) proposed a similar unsupervised technique for mapping recipe instructions to actions based on a hard Expectation Maximization algorithm and a restricted set of verb argument types (*location, object*).

In the paradigm of semantic role labeling, the approach of (Malmaud et al., 2014) uses a Markov decision process where ingredients and utensils are propagated over the temporal order of instructions and where the context information is stored in a latent vector which disambiguates and augments the instruction statement under analysis. The context information corresponds to the state of the kitchen and integrates the changes of this state according to the evolving recipe instructions. It yields a good performance for the instruction analysis.

In the case based reasoning paradigm, (Dufour-Lussier et al., 2012) represent the cooking instructions as a work-flow and thus propose a method for the automatic acquisition of a rich case representation of cooking recipes for process-oriented case-based reasoning from free recipe text. The cooking process is represented using the Allen (Allen, 1981) algebra extended with relations over interval durations. After applying classical NLP tools for segmentation, part-of speech tagging, syntactic analysis, the extraction process from texts focuses on the anaphora resolution and verb argument analysis. The actions are modeled on the basis of the instructional text *without* considering the implicit information proper to the cooking recipes. The underlying knowledge resource is the case-based reasoning system Taaable (Cordier et al., 2014). The existing methods of cuisine texts analysis converge on the necessity to have a richer context around the terms present in the input text. Various approaches have been proposed to provide such context. Some of them propose specific meta-languages such as MILK[10] (Tasse and Smith, 2008) or SIMMR (Jermsurawong and Habash, 2015)[11]. MILK has been proposed as a machine-readable target language to create sets of instructions that represent the actions demanded by the recipe statements. It is is based on the first-order logic, but allows handling the temporal order as well as creation/deletion of ingredients. A small corpus of 250 recipes has been manually annotated using MILK (CURD (Carnegie Mellon University Recipe Database)). Similarly, SIMMR (Jermsurawong and Habash, 2015) allows to represent a recipe as a dependency tree. The leaves of the tree are the recipe ingredients and its internal nodes are the recipe instructions. MILK tags have been used to construct the SIMMR trees. Machine learning methods (SVM[12] classification) have then been used for instruction-ingredient linking, instruction-instruction linking using SIMMR. Other approaches for getting more context for the cooking recipe analysis are dynamic data structures (i.e. latent vector used by (Malmaud et al., 2014)) and graph-shaped resources (ontologies, semantic networks) as in our case.

[10]*Minimal Instruction Language for the Kitchen.*
[11]*Simplified Ingredient Merging Map in Recipes.*
[12]Support Vector Machine Classification.

3 Preliminaries

The dietary restrictions are defined as follows: *Diabetes*, *GlutenFree*, *Halal*, *Hindu*, *Kosher* , *LowCalories*, *LowFat*, *LactoseFree*, *LowSalt*, *Vegan*, *Vegetarian*. For these diets, we automatically extracted and manually validated an initial set of approximately 200 forbidden ingredients. We used domain-specific resources (lists of ingredients) found on the Web for this step. These ingredients (if not already present in our graph-based knowledge resource) have been encoded as nodes and linked to the nodes representing the diets listed above by the arcs typed *r_incompatible*. The nutritional restrictions differ in terms of their semantic structure (which may rely on composition (*part-whole* relation), cutting types (*holonymy* etc.), cooking state (i.e. boiled carrots are undesirable in case of diabetes).

3.1 Corpus and Knowledge Resource

For our experiment we used a set of 5,000 dish titles in French, which corresponds to a corpus[13]. of 19,000 words and a vocabulary of 2,900 terms (after removing stop words and irrelevant expressions such as "tarte tatin *à ma façon*", *tarte tatin my way*). This data mirrors the French urban culinary tradition as well as the established practice of searching the Web for recipes. The data scarcity proper to the recipe titles is an important obstacle to their processing. Distributional scores used by (Hua et al., 2015) and (Beltagy et al., 2014) may be interesting in terms of flavor associations, but they also demonstrate that we need to know more about the most likely semantic neighborhood of the term to handle the part-whole semantics and incompatibility analysis.

The semantic resource we use for the experiments is the RezoJDM lexical semantic network for French [14]. This resource stems from the game with a purpose AI project JeuxDeMots (Lafourcade, 2007). Built and constantly improved by crowd-sourcing (games with a purpose, direct contribution), RezoJDM is a directed, typed, and weighted graph. Today it contains 1.4M nodes and 90M relations divided into more than 100 types. The structural properties of the network have been detailed in (Lafourcade, 2011) and later in (Chatzikyriakidis et al., 2015), its inference and annotation mechanisms respectively by (Zarrouk et al., 2013) and (Ramadier, 2016). The ever ending process of graph population is carried on using different techniques including games with a purpose, crowd-sourcing, mapping to other semantic and knowledge resources such as Wikipedia or BabelNet (Navigli and Ponzetto, 2012). In addition, endogenous inference mechanisms, introduced by (Zarrouk et al., 2013) are also used to populate the graph. They rely on the transitivity of the *is-a*, *hyponym*, and *synonym* relationships and are built for handling polysemy. In addition to the hierarchical relation types, RezoJDM contains grammatical(*part-of-speech*), causal, thematic relations as well as relations of generativist flavor (ex. *telic role*). This resource is considered as a closed world i.e. every information that is not present in the graph is assumed as false.

It has been shown by (Ramadier, 2016) that, for the sake of precision, general and domain specific knowledge should not be separated. Thus, for our experiment we immerse nutrition, sensory, technical knowledge into RezoJDM to enhance the coverage of the graph. This has been done partly through the direct contribution. External resources such as domain specific lexicons and terminological resources have been used. In particular, some equivalence and synonym relation triples have been extracted from IATE[15] term base[16]. The Agrovoc[17] thesaurus provided only a few new terms; it contained no relevant relations. Additionally, as RezoJDM can be enhanced using crowd-sourcing methods and, in particular, games with a purpose, specific game with a purpose assignments have been given to the JeuxDeMots (contribution interface for RezoJDM) players. Today (June 2017) the domain specific subgraph corresponds to 40K terms (approximately 2.8% of the RezoJDM). The overall adaptation process took about 3 weeks.

In the framework of our experiment, we use *taxonomy* relations, *part-whole* relations, *object-mater* relations and, in some cases, *hyponymy* and *characteristic* relations. Running the experiment involved preprocessing steps (multi-word terms detection, lemmatization, disambiguation), browsing

[13] The corpus has been collected from the following Web resources : *15%* `www.cuisineaz.fr`, *20%* `www.cuisinelibre.org` *et 65%* `www.allrecipe.fr`

[14] `http://www.jeuxdemots.org/jdm-about.php`

[15] `http://iate.europa.eu/switchLang.do?success=mainPagelang=fr`

[16] The part of the IATE resource that has been used corresponds to the subject field 6006.

[17] `http://aims.fao.org/fr/agrovoc`

the graph following path constraints, scoring possible incompatibilities, and possibly normalizing scores. Among other approaches using a similar plot, (Poria et al., 2014) use ConceptNet (Liu and Singh, 2004) network for the semantic analysis task.

4 Method

The preprocessing step includes text segmentation which relies on the multi-word lexical entities detection, followed by stop-words removal. The multi-word term detection is done in two steps. First, the recipe titles are cut into n-grams using a dynamic-length sliding window ($2 \leq 4$). Second, the segments are compared to the lexical entries present in RezoJDM which is therefore used as a dictionary. In RezoJDM, the multi-word terms are related to their "parts" by the relation typed *locution* (or "phrase"). This relation is useful for compound terms analysis. Bi-grams and trigrams are the most frequent structures in the domain-specific subgraph as well as in RezoJDM. Indeed, they represent respectively 28% and 16% of the overall set of multi-word terms and expressions (300K units). For our experiment, we often opted for trigrams which turned out to be more informative (i.e. correspond to nodes with a higher out degree).

French (*English*)
1. Carpe à_la_forestière (*Forest_style carp*)
2. Carré d'agneau dans_son_jus (*Rack of lamb in_its_own_jus*)
3. Waterzoí de lieu_noir (*Coley waterzoof*)
4. Verrines de lentilles au saumon_fumé (*Lentil and smoked_salmon verrines*)
5. Gâteau_basque à la confiture de cerises_noires (*Basque_cake with black_cherry jam*)

Table 2: Preprocessed recipe titles. Expressions relevant for the domain (1,2) as well as multi-word terms (3,4), and phrases(5) are detected. Sometimes, two segmentations are possible for the same input. In such cases, the contrast is favored by exploring syntactic features and outgoing semantic relationships of terms in RezoJDM.

4.1 From Text to Graph

Starting from a sequence $w_1, w_2, ...w_n$ of n terms, we build a *context* namely the lemmatized and disambiguated representation of the recipe title under scope. Such *context* is the entry point to our knowledge resource.

A *context* is a sequence of nodes (the text order is preserved) : $C_{w_1,w_2,...w_n} = n_{w_1}, n_{w_2}, ...n_{w_n}$ where the node n_{w_n} is the most precise syntactic and semantic representation of the surface form available in RezoJDM. To obtain such representation we search for the node corresponding to the surface form if it exists[18]. Then, we yield its refinement if the term is polysemic. The irrelevant refinements are discriminated using a list of key terms that define our domain (i.e. thematic subgraph within a lexical semantic network). The identification of the refinement is done through the cascade processing of relationships of a node typed *refinement*, *domain*, and *meaning*. The context creation function returns for *quiche au thon et aux tomates* (*quiche with tuna and tomatos*) the result *[quiche (préparation culinaire), thon (poisson,chair), tomate légume-fruit]*, respectively:"quiche (preparation), tuna (fish flesh), tomato (fruit-vegetable))". For each node $n_i \in C$ we explore paths $S = ((n_1 a_r n_2), (n_2 a_r n_3), (n_{m-1} a_r n_m))$. The type of relationships we choose for the graph traversal depends on the local category of the node:

1. If $isa("preparation", n_i)$[19], $r \in \{hypo, part-whole, matter\}$.
   This is the case of mixtures, dishes and other complex ingredients;

2. If $isa("ingredient", n_i)$[20], $r \in \{isa, syn, part-whole, matter, charac\}$.
   It is the case of plain ingredients like *tomato*.

The weight of all relations we traverse must be strictly positive. We traverse the graph testing a range of conditions: relevance to the domain of interest D_{alim} (food domain), existence of a path of a certain length (≤ 2) and type between the candidate node and and the rest of the *Context* under analysis, co-meronymy relation etc.

To obtain relevant results, two conditions are to be fulfilled. First, there must be a disambiguation strategy and a domain filtering. Second, the similarity has to be handled between the $preparation$ and its hyponyms. Indeed, the exploration of the *part-whole* relations of the network refers to *all the possible* ingredients and constituents

[18] In the opposite case the acquisition process through external resources like Wikipedia, Web and through crowdsourcing (Games with a purpose) may be triggered (if an open world hypothesis is favored).

[19] *First Order Logic Notation.*

[20] *Idem.*

of the $preparation$. If the $preparation$ has a conceptual role (i.e. "cake"), the *part-whole* relations analysis will output a lot of noise. In our example, it is important to grasp the absence of *pork (meat)* and the presence of *tuna (fish)* in the *quiche* under scope. Therefore, instead of directly exploring the *part-whole* relations of the $quiche(preparation)$, we rather try to find similar $quiche(preparation)$ hyponyms for the context *C*="quiche (preparation), tuna (fish flesh), tomato (fruit-vegetable))" and yield the typical parts they have in common with the generic $quiche(preparation)$. Our function finds the hyponym which maximizes the similarity score. This score is a normalized Jaccard index over all the positive outgoing *part-whole*, *isa*, *matter* relations.
$J(S_C, S_{C_{hypo}}) = \frac{S_C \cap S_{C_{hypo}}}{S_C \cup S_{C_{hypo}}}$ where C_{hypo} is the *hyponym context* built on the go.
Different threshold values have been experimented. Empirically, the threshold fixed at 0.30 allows capturing generic similarities such as (for our example) *quiche saumon courgette* ("quiche salmon zucchini") score=0.32, a quiche with some fish and a vegetable. More precise similarity corresponds to higher scores.
Using the described strategy, the irrelevant recipes such as *quiche lorraine* (score=0.20) are efficiently discriminated. Once the relevant hyponym is identified, its *part-whole* neighbors can be grasped. A specific graph traversal strategy is used for the LowSalt diet. It includes exploring the *characteristic* relation type for the $preparation$ and its parts.

4.2 From Graph to Incompatibilities

The incompatibility calculation takes as input the list of diets and the queue F containing terms related to main context. This function looks for an dietary incompatibility path S_{inc} such that $N' \in F$ $\wedge$ $S_{inc} = ((N', r_{type}, N), (N, r_{inc}, N_{DIET}))$ $\wedge$ $type \in (holo|isa|haspart|substance|hypo)$. The output is a key value pair (*diet*, *score*). The score depends on the distance in the RezoJDM graph and on the relation type between the diet and the incompatible node in the context. Besides the *refinement* relation type[21], it is calculated as follows for the distance $d : \frac{1}{1+d}$. The score for the whole context corresponds to the addition of the individual scores of the context nodes. It is adapted in order to bring it closer to a probability distribution and allow further statistical or predictive processing. Our system first obtains a list of nodes linked to the context (see 3.1). After following a traversal strategy, it returns a list of probabilistic scores for each part of the context. I.e. (w corresponds to $weight$ and d corresponds to $distance$) :

```
recipe : quiche thon tomate
quiche>preparation,thon>poisson,
tomate>legume
```

Further follows similarity processing as described in 3.2., then processing of parts shared by quiche and its hyponyms similar to the context. For each part, the *isa*, *part-whole*, *mater* and *characteristic* relations are further explored

`r_has_part pte d=1 w=6` **dough**
`r_has_part oeufs d=1 w=105` **eggs** etc.

Intermediate raw scores are returned (example : $quiche(preparation)$):

```
Diabetes 1.3, LactoseFree 3.0, Halal 0.0,
Kosher 0.3, LowCalories 1.5, LowSalt 0.5,
GlutenFree 1.8, Hindu 0.5, LowFat 0.8,
Vegan 0.5, Vegetarian 0.3
```

Same processing is performed for all the other nodes from the context. The output summarizes scores per ingredient and per diet. It can be "normalized" according to the following rule applied to the raw score in order to $s \in L_s$ (raw list of scores) in order to produce a probabilistic score s_p : if $s \geq 0.5$, $s_p \leftarrow 1$, if $s \leq 0.5$, $s_p \leftarrow 0.5$. The range of this new score is restricted to three values : compatible (0), uncertain (0.5), and incompatible (1).

```
final probabilistic scores
for "quiche thon tomate"
Diabetes 0.5, LactoseFree 1.0, Halal 0.0,
Kosher 0.5, LowCalories 1.0, LowSalt 1.0,
GlutenFree 1.0, Hindu 1.0, LowFat 1.0,
Vegan 1.0, Vegetarian 1.0
```

In a restaurant scenario, a client would be informed about the strict incompatibility or

[21]Which participates to the disambiguation process.

compatibility of a dish with his or her nutritional restrictions and alerted about some potential incompatibilities that would need further information from the caterer. The list of terms that are not present in the resource (for example, *sibnekh, zwiebelkuchen*) is output by the system. It serves to the further improvement of the RezoJDM graph from external resources.

4.3 Evaluation and Discussion

The system has been evaluated using a incompatibility annotated corpus of 1,500 recipe titles. The evaluation data has been partially collected using structured document retrieval simultaneously with the raw corpus constitution. Relevant metatags (HTML tags present in micro-formats[22]) have been used to pre-build incompatibility scores. The overlap between the different diets (vegan recipes are compatible with a vegetarian diet etc.) has been taken into account. The labels have been adjusted and enriched (LawSalt, Kosher diets) by hand by the author because the structured metatags do not contain such information. The obtained evaluation scores are binary. Our system is under improvement, we estimated that the score returned by the system should be $\geq$ 0.5 to be ranked as acceptable. Later, a finer grained evaluation will be adopted.

Our results expressed in terms of precision, recall and f-measure (F1 score) are listed in Table 4. The most important score is the precision as, for an allergic or intolerant restaurant customer, even a very small quantity of a forbidden product may be dangerous. The average value correspond to the macro-average (arithmetic mean), F-score average is therefore the harmonic mean of precision average rate and recall average rate.

For the halal diet, there are very few terms in the graph that point to this diet. The *low calories* and *vegetarian* diets are well known among the RezoJDM community and well represented in the graph. In 13% of cases, the graph traversal did not return any result as the terms corresponding to the words of the context do not exist in the graph. It was the case of borrowings (such as *quinotto*) or lexical creations[23] (i.e. *anti-tiramisu* as our analysis scheme doesn't take into account morphology). The average number of incompatibility scores $\neq 0$ per recipe title is of about 3.8. Traditional diets (such as halal diet and kosher diet) have been very challenging as the nature of nutritional restriction for them may concern food associations. The low salt diet incompatibility detection is still difficult because salt is everywhere and it is sometimes difficult to find a criterion to separate the property from the possibility of being salted.

Given the specificity of our resource, a low score may depend on the lack of some relevant information in the graph. Thus, the output may be considered as correct (at least at the development stage) but with a low "confidence" which corresponds to a lower mean[24] value.

	Corpus (scores)		
Diet	**0**	**0.5**	**1**
Diabetes	344	1,667	2,989
LactoseFree	1,410	1,856	1,733
Halal	1,629	3,140	231
Kosher	1,307	3,453	240
LowCalories	2,540	122	2,338
LowSalt	3,491	1,312	197
GlutenFree	589	2,961	1,450
Hindu	568	3,939	493
LowFat	2,161	2,636	203
Vegan	454	4,261	285
Vegetarian	360	1,655	2,985
totals	**14,852**	**27,004**	**13,144**

Table 3: Repartition between the 3 possible probabilistic scores in the whole corpus.

	Evaluation set		
Diet	**Precision**	**Recall**	**F1 score**
Diabetes	92%	92%	92%
LactoseFree	71%	73%	72%
Halal	65%	75%	70%
Kosher	67%	60%	63%
LowCalories	60%	75%	67%
LowSalt	88%	65%	75%
GlutenFree	80%	73%	76%
Hindu	86%	80%	83%
LowFat	67%	70%	68%
Vegan	80%	90%	85%
Vegetarian	83%	90%	86%
macro-average	**76%**	**77%**	**76%**

Table 4: Corpus-based evaluation. We specify the repartition between the 3 possible probabilistic scores in the whole corpus and detail the quality of our scoring for an sub-corpus annotated for evaluation. The evaluation set is a subset of our corpus annotated in incompatibilities. We totally ignore the annotations during the processing.

[22] Micro-formats(μF) refer to standardized semantic markup of web-pages.

[23] The term *lexical creation* refers to the neology (creation of new terms).

[24] The mean, as it is understood here, weights each score s_i according to its probability given the dataset, s_i. Thus, $\mu = \sum s_i p_i$.

The mean (M) and standard deviation (SD) values reveal this confidence issue (Table 5). A low M value together with a low SD indicates that there were too many uncertain scores (≤ 0.5) among the resulting scores of a particular diet. On the contrary, $M \geq 0.5$ and $SD \leq 0.5$ reveal a good confidence about the incompatibility. in the case of "no salt" diet, very few incompatibilities have been detected with low confidence, thus finer grained approach is needed (i.e. relationship annotation). In the case of GlutenFree and LowCalories the scores are quite confident but sparse : the data is unequally distributed in the resource, more relationship types should be explored. the overall M and SD values reveal low confidence but uniform scores. To maximize the confidence related to the score, the knowledge resource must be continuously enhanced. Today this is achieved using two main strategies: exogenous and endogenous. The first one may include term extraction from corpora, relationship identification based on word embeddings, direct contribution, specific games with a purpose assignments. The second one refers to propagation of the relations already existing in the graph using inference schemes based on the transitivity of the *isa*, *part-whole*, and *synonym* semantic relations as proposed by (Zarrouk et al., 2013). Using a lexical semantic network for text processing offers some clear advantages. First, there is no need to use multiple data structures during the processing. Second, the graph structure supports encoding various kinds of information that can be useful for text processing tasks. Every piece of information encoded using the graph formalism is machine interpretable and can be accessed during the traversal. Finally, the graph based analysis strategy has an explanatory feature,

Diet	M	SD
Diabetes	0.785	0.295
LactoseFree	0.200	0.215
Halal	0.240	0.239
Kosher	0.275	0.243
LowCalories	0.487	0.484
LowSalt	0.031	0.094
GlutenFree	0.549	0.349
Hindu	0.447	0.244
LowFat	0.380	0.202
Vegan	0.406	0.219
Vegetarian	0.809	0.253
overall	**0.406**	**0.219**

Table 5: Mean values per diet (evaluation)

it is always possible to know why the system returned some particular output. However, two main issues must be tackled : the knowledge resource **population** method and the **filtering** strategy while traversing the resource. To test the portability of the approach, we run it using the ConceptNet common knowledge network and a restricted set of aligned recipe titles in English and French. The obtained scores have been compared across languages. They are given as follows in our example: "score for French [score for English]".

```
"blanquette de veau" ["veal blanquette"]
Vegan 1.0[0.5],Vegetarian 1.0[0.5]
Hindu 1.0[0.5],Diabetes 0.6[0.0],
LowLactose 0.5[0.0],Kosher 0.4[0.0],
LowFat 0.4[0.0], LowSalt 0.4[0.0]
```

Thus, the portability of the method is proportional to the quantity of available resources that can be assimilated to human contribution (i.e.corpora of user contributed recipes for a given language) and to the amount of direct human expert or non expert contribution.

5 Conclusion

We introduced the use of a lexical-semantic network for dietary conflict detection based on dish titles. The scores obtained by our system can be used for building specific resources for machine learning tasks such as classifier training. Among the perspectives, we can list :

- knowledge resource population using external resources and endogenous approaches ;
- mapping the resource to other existing semantic resources;
- making the system evolve towards a multilingual (language independent?) dietary conflict detection.

An important advantage of the system over purely statistical approaches is its explanatory feature, we can always know how the system came to its decision and thus can constantly improve it. The limitations of our contribution are linked to its improvement model which is based on contribution work and the necessity to (weakly) validate the new relations.

References

Yong-Yeol Ahn, Sebastian E. Ahnert, James P. Bagrow, and Albert-Lszl Barabsi. 2011. Flavor network and the principles of food pairing. *CoRR* abs/1111.6074.

James F. Allen. 1981. An interval-based representation of temporal knowledge. In *Proceedings of the 7th International Joint Conference on Artificial Intelligence, IJCAI '81, Vancouver, BC, Canada, August 24-28, 1981*. pages 221–226.

I. Beltagy, Katrin Erk, and Raymond Mooney. 2014. Semantic parsing using distributional semantics and probabilistic logic. In *Proceedings of ACL 2014 Workshop on Semantic Parsing (SP-2014)*. Baltimore, MD, pages 7–11.

Johan Bos. 2015. Open-domain semantic parsing with boxer. In *Proceedings of the 20th Nordic Conference of Computational Linguistics, NODALIDA 2015, May 11-13, 2015, Institute of the Lithuanian Language, Vilnius, Lithuania*. pages 301–304.

Stergios Chatzikyriakidis, Mathieu Lafourcade, Lionel Ramadier, and Manel Zarrouk. 2015. Type Theories and Lexical Networks: Using Serious Games as the Basis for Multi-Sorted Typed Systems. In *ESSLLI: European Summer School in Logic, Language and Information*. Barcelona, Spain.

Amélie Cordier, Valmi Dufour-Lussier, Jean Lieber, Emmanuel Nauer, Fadi Badra, Julien Cojan, Emmanuelle Gaillard, Laura Infante-Blanco, Pascal Molli, Amedeo Napoli, and Hala Skaf-Molli. 2014. Taaable: a Case-Based System for personalized Cooking. In Stefania Montani and Lakhmi C. Jain, editors, *Successful Case-based Reasoning Applications-2*, Springer, volume 494 of *Studies in Computational Intelligence*, pages 121–162.

Valmi Dufour-Lussier, Florence Le Ber, Jean Lieber, Thomas Meilender, and Emmanuel Nauer. 2012. Semi-automatic annotation process for procedural texts: An application on cooking recipes. *CoRR* abs/1209.5663.

Christiane Fellbaum, editor. 1998. *WordNet An Electronic Lexical Database*. The MIT Press, Cambridge, MA ; London.

J. R. Firth. 1957. A synopsis of linguistic theory 1930-55. 1952-59:1–32.

Wen Hua, Zhongyuan Wang, Haixun Wang, Kai Zheng, and Xiaofang Zhou. 2015. Short text understanding through lexical-semantic analysis. In Johannes Gehrke, Wolfgang Lehner, Kyuseok Shim, Sang Kyun Cha, and Guy M. Lohman, editors, *ICDE*. IEEE Computer Society, pages 495–506.

Jermsak Jermsurawong and Nizar Habash. 2015. Predicting the structure of cooking recipes. In Llus Mrquez, Chris Callison-Burch, Jian Su, Daniele Pighin, and Yuval Marton, editors, *EMNLP*. The Association for Computational Linguistics, pages 781–786.

Chlo Kiddon, Ganesa Thandavam Ponnuraj, Luke Zettlemoyer, and Yejin Choi. 2015. *Mise en place: Unsupervised interpretation of instructional recipes*. Association for Computational Linguistics (ACL), pages 982–992.

Mathieu Lafourcade. 2007. Making people play for Lexical Acquisition with the JeuxDeMots prototype. In *SNLP'07: 7th International Symposium on Natural Language Processing*. Pattaya, Chonburi, Thailand, page 7.

Mathieu Lafourcade. 2011. *Lexicon and semantic analysis of texts - structures, acquisition, computation and games with words*. Habilitation à diriger des recherches, Université Montpellier II - Sciences et Techniques du Languedoc.

H. Liu and P. Singh. 2004. Conceptnet — a practical commonsense reasoning tool-kit. *BT Technology Journal* 22(4):211–226.

Jonathan Malmaud, Earl Wagner, Nancy Chang, and Kevin Murphy. 2014. Cooking with semantics. In *Proceedings of the ACL 2014 Workshop on Semantic Parsing*. Association for Computational Linguistics, Baltimore, MD, pages 33–38.

Shinsuke Mori, Tetsuro Sasada, Yoko Yamakata, and Koichiro Yoshino. 2012. A machine learning approach to recipe text processing.

Roberto Navigli and Simone Paolo Ponzetto. 2012. BabelNet: The automatic construction, evaluation and application of a wide-coverage multilingual semantic network. *Artificial Intelligence* 193:217–250.

Soujanya Poria, Basant Agarwal, Alexander Gelbukh, Amir Hussain, and Newton Howard. 2014. *Dependency-Based Semantic Parsing for Concept-Level Text Analysis*, Springer Berlin Heidelberg, Berlin, Heidelberg, pages 113–127.

Lionel Ramadier. 2016. *Indexation and learning of terms and relations from reports of radiology*. Theses, Université de Montpellier.

Dan Tasse and Noah A. Smith. 2008. Sour cream:toward semantic processing of recipes. *T.R. CMU-LTI-08-005* page 9.

Manel Zarrouk, Mathieu Lafourcade, and Alain Joubert. 2013. Inference and Reconciliation in a Crowdsourced Lexical-Semantic Network. In *CICLING: International Conference on Intelligent Text Processing and Computational Linguistics*. Samos, Greece, 14th.

Analysing Market Sentiments: Utilising Deep Learning to Exploit Relationships within the Economy

Tobias Daudert
Insight Centre for Data Analytics, National University of Ireland Galway
tobias.daudert@insight-centre.org

Abstract

In today's world, globalisation is not only affecting inter-culturalism but also linking markets across the globe. Given that all markets are affecting each other and are not only driven by fundamental data but also by sentiments, sentiment analysis regarding the markets becomes a tool to predict, anticipate, and milden future economic crises such as the one we faced in 2008. In this paper, an approach to improve sentiment analysis by exploiting relationships among different kinds of sentiment, together with supplementary information, from and across various data sources is proposed.

1 Introduction

Nowadays, modern societies and their welfare depend on market economies with the financial markets at the heart. This means that millions of people around the globe are affected by changes in the markets (Khadjeh Nassirtoussi et al., 2014). The financial markets are not only driven by fundamental factors (e.g. trends in GDP, inflation, employment, monetary and fiscal policy) but also by psychology-related factors such as public mood. This behaviour can be observed in economic bubbles which indicate irrational and emotional actions of the market participants (Khadjeh Nassirtoussi et al., 2014). In today's increasingly complex global economy, more sophisticated approaches are needed to provide better insights and prevent future economic crises (Khadjeh Nassirtoussi et al., 2014). Therefore, it is important to understand what the markets, particularly the financial markets as a proxy for the market economies, are influenced by, how they react, and how strong the influence is.

Given the existence of different sentiments and alternative data all affecting each other, an experimental approach to exploit their relations is proposed. The aim of this approach is to derive additional information from different data types in order to improve sentiment analysis. In this paper, we outline the proposal and detail its components, focusing on its fine-grained construction to exploit contextual sentiments in microblogs data and news data individually, as well as their mutual relationships.

2 Background

Within the last 17 years, sentiment analysis aiming at measuring public mood in respect of the financial domain grew to an important field of research. Liu (2015) defines sentiment analysis, synonymously called opinion mining, as "the field of study that analyses people's opinions, sentiments, appraisals, attitudes, and emotions toward entities and their attributes expressed in written text". Market sentiment is defined as "the feeling or tone of a market, or its crowd psychology".[1] Prior research has shown how sentiments and opinions can affect market dynamics, thus, making the financial domain a high-impact case study for sentiment analysis in text (Goonatilake and Herath, 2007; Van De Kauter et al., 2015). Sentiments are extracted from various sources of data, such as news. Within this source, one can find discussions regarding macroeconomic factors, company-specific reports, or political information, which

[1] http://www.investopedia.com/terms/m/marketsentiment.asp

Proceedings of the Student Research Workshop associated with RANLP 2017, pages 10–16,
Varna, Bulgaria, 4-6 September 2017.
http://doi.org/10.26615/issn.1314-9156.2017_002

can be relevant to the market (Sinha, 2014). Good news tends to lift markets and increase optimism, bad news tend to lower markets (Schuster, 2003; Van De Kauter et al., 2015). As an example, Bollen et al. (2010) showed that changes in public mood reflect value shifts in the Dow Jones Industrial Index three to four days later. Additionally, evidence has been found that both quantitative measures (e.g. the quantity of news, market fluctuation) and qualitative indicators, (e.g. linguistic style and tone) affect investors' behaviour (Loughran and Mcdonald, 2011; Takala et al., 2010; Tetlock et al., 2008). Given the link between sentiment and market dynamics, the analysis of public sentiment becomes a powerful method to predict the market reaction. Despite its active improvement over the past 17 years, the field of sentiment analysis with regard to the markets is not thoroughly explored. The relationship between textual and investor sentiment is complex and it is unclear to what extent they affect each other and how much each of them affects the markets (Kearney and Liu, 2014). The quality of interpreting such sentiment can determine the predictability of the financial markets. Thus, researchers have started targeting this problem lately. However, no well-rounded theoretical and technical framework exists (Khadjeh Nassirtoussi et al., 2014). Dedicated Natural Language Processing (NLP) approaches for analysing investor's behaviour are non-existent at all (Kumar and Ravi, 2016). This is partially due to the interdisciplinary nature of the field since it combines economics, computer science and natural language processing (Khadjeh Nassirtoussi et al., 2014). NLP and computer science researchers generally lack the economics background and are too technically-focused whereas researchers with an economics background are lacking the knowledge to develop profound language processing tools. The current state of the art is based on lacking research in multiple sub-fields which are related but not exclusive to: 1) linguistic issues; 2) data type and data sourcing problems; 3) narrow research focus; 4) different sentiment types; and 5) generally accepted and available benchmark data, and evaluation methods. Below, each of the issues identified are detailed.

2.1 Linguistic Issues

Research effort is required to overcome and address complex linguistic issues such as sarcasm, irony, and poorly-structured and/or colloquial language. More syntax-based techniques such as parse-trees for pattern recognition require more attention (Khadjeh Nassirtoussi et al., 2014). Additionally, the process of content analysis is still in need of more authoritative and field-specific dictionaries (Kearney and Liu, 2014). On the side of semantics, aspect-level approaches can be used to provide a richer sentiment analysis (Schouten and Frasincar, 2016). Furthermore, the construction of more and improved customised ontologies are required to tackle the problem of text classification with a higher accuracy in each domain. In the case of the features used, researchers currently focus on word occurrence methods (Khadjeh Nassirtoussi et al., 2014; Kumar and Ravi, 2016). However, additional value could be added using abstraction for feature reduction or weighting schemes for semantic compression. All this leads to machine learning-based sentiment analysis approaches with low accuracy results (Takala et al., 2010).

2.2 Data Type and Data Sourcing Issues

Most of the present research is only based on specific data sources such as financial or corporate news. To overcome this threshold, it could be fruitful to combine "qualitative information from textual sentiment into equity asset pricing models [..] as publicly available documents or media articles may contain additional hard-to-quantify information" (Kearney and Liu, 2014; Kumar and Ravi, 2016). As textual sentiment in articles, blogs, or posts mostly reflects opinion, it would not only be of additional value to use these types of textual data together with fundamental figures but also to integrate technical signals such as the moving average convergence divergence (MACD) or the relative strength index (RSI) as additional features into machine learning approaches dealing with public sentiment. Only a few researchers (Butler and Kešelj, 2009; Hagenau et al., 2013; Rachlin et al., 2007; Schumaker and Chen, 2009;

Schumaker et al., 2012; Zhai et al., 2007) have experimented with such a hybrid approach. Their findings are promising; most of the researchers could improve the accuracy of their classifiers by using additional, non-textual data. As an example, Zhai et al. (2007) used news, divided into company specific news and general market news, together with stock price information and stock price based calculated trading indicators. The results show the highest accuracy for the approach combining all available information as presented in Figure 1. Only Rachlin et al. (2007) could not achieve the highest accuracy using a joint approach; they achieved the best results only based on stock prices and from stock price generated indicators. In contrast to the proposed research in this paper, all the works mentioned are purely focusing on stock price prediction. Different data is used to achieve a higher accuracy on stock price forecasts instead of using the multitude of information to additionally improve the textual sentiment classifier itself. The textual sentiment, or media sentiment as described in section 2.4, used as input to their proposed models is not the same sentiment their predictions, as output, are referring to. For example, Schumaker et al. (2012) is claiming that a correlation between textual sentiment, news, and stock prices exists but a possible influence of stock prices on textual sentiment remains unexplored.

Data sets	Accuracy (%)
Price	58.8
Direct news	62.5
Indirect news	50.0
Combined news	64.7
Price & News	70.1

Figure 1: Prediction Accuracy as achieved by Zhai et al. (2007)

However, online postings bear challenges given their informal writing nature which significantly differs from professionally written media articles or corporate documents (Kearney and Liu, 2014). Text short in length (such as microblog messages) can be quite opinionated, dense in information, dependent on the modelling of economic context, and challenging to parse due to the different vocabularies used (Sinha, 2014). In addition, there are still qualitative information sources that have not been widely studied yet. Examples include business and political speeches, blogs, television news videos, and various social media platforms (Kearney and Liu, 2014). Many of the works to date are based on the specific news sources such as financial or corporate news (Kumar and Ravi, 2016).

2.3 Narrow Research Focus

Most of the work in this area is focused on specific companies (Kearney and Liu, 2014; Kumar and Ravi, 2016). Similar methodologies can be applied to other markets such as bonds, commodities, or derivatives which are potentially driven by public mood to a variable extent. Given the desire to address the general market sentiment, an overly narrow focus on individual markets is misleading since all markets are interfering with each other. Hence, it is necessary to not only study the U.S. markets but to consider additional markets linked to different languages such as German. To identify and track this dependence, short and long-term studies regarding sentiment changes are required. However, the majority of the research only considers the news article time of release (Kumar and Ravi, 2016).

2.4 Different Sentiment Types

Current research is not taking different types of sentiment and their interference into account. The different sentiments include public sentiments (e.g. Twitter, Facebook), media sentiments (e.g. Wall Street Journal, Financial Times), expert sentiments (e.g. analysts, investors), and company sentiments (e.g. Annual reports, CEO's interviews). These sentiments are highly contextual and expressed in different formats (Khadjeh Nassirtoussi et al., 2014).

2.5 Generally Accepted and Available Benchmark Data

The availability of experimental data and benchmarks for sentiment analysis in the financial domain is currently very limited. Most of the researchers have accumulated their own datasets

(Khadjeh Nassirtoussi et al., 2014) leading to fragmented datasets and raising issues with the reproducibility of experiments. It is not only important to choose the right data sources and experimental approach but also to consider the fundamental groundwork in this area of research. The lack of benchmark datasets which was addressed by Kumar and Ravi (2016) leads to predictions useless for comparison. Here, a common framework would provide a remedy.

3 Methodology

In order to tackle some of the issues mentioned in Section 2, the proposed research is aiming at the exploitation of different sentiments contained in different data types and sources. At minimum, two different data types, microblogs (i.e. Twitter and Stocktwits) as well as financial news articles will be used, and it will be explored whether they can be used to improve the accuracy of each other's sentiment analysis.[2][3] The proposed methodology is presented in Figure 2. The goal of this fine-grained sentiment analysis pipeline is to utilise supplementary information from and across different data sources. Microblogs and articles published close to each other in time might contain additional information relevant to both and potentially increase the accuracy of the sentiment analysis of the two. In order to exploit data type specific features, dedicated sentiment analysis methods for microblogs as well as financial articles will be developed. I believe data specific sentiment analysers lead to the most accurate sentiments analysis.

3.1 Data Stream

The data that will be used as input for the proposed experiment comprises a collection of 100 million Tweets derived from tracking 1,588 keywords on Twitter, and 25,000 financial news articles from various sources such as Bloomberg, Investopedia, and CNN Money.[4][5][6] Initially, experiments will be based on textual data in English language, however, German data will be considered at a later stage. The collected data is currently stored in MongoDB due to its flexibility with different data structures and, therefore, storage optimisation.[7] The size of the collection amounts to 465 GB.

3.2 Processing Stream

The processing stream consists of 3 components: the Microblog Analyser, the News Analyser, and the Sentiment Aggregator which are detailed below.

3.2.1 Microblog Analyser

The Microblog Analyser is a tool dedicated to analysing sentiment in microblogs using deep learning (DL) (LeCun et al., 2015). It will be implemented using PyTorch and generate a document-level sentiment within the range from -1 (very negative) to +1 (very positive) with 0 as neutral, using aspect-level sentiment analysis.[8] DL has been chosen based on the performance shown in recent research in the area of sentiment analysis related to finance such as during the Semeval 2017 Task 5 (Cortis et al., 2017), in which most of the top ranked teams applied either pure DL or hybrid approaches utilising DL together with lexica or ontologies. In addition, there are still many insights yet to become concerning aspect-level sentiment analysis (Wang et al., 2016). The decision in favor of PyTorch is made due to my experience in Python and its support by Facebook, Twitter, and NVIDIA. Initially, publicly available Twitter gold standards (GS) such as the Semeval 2017 Task 5 one (Cortis et al., 2017) comprising 2494 Tweets will be used for training and testing. This GS will be replaced by a newly created, more problem-specific gold standard only focusing on entities tracked on Twitter.

3.2.2 News Analyser

The News Analyser is similar to the Microblog Analyser. It is dedicated to analyse sentiment in financial news articles also using deep learning implemented with PyTorch, for the same reasons as described in 3.2.1. Financial news articles will be annotated manually for the creation of a gold

[2] http://www.twitter.com/
[3] http://www.stocktwits.com/
[4] http://www.bloomberg.com/
[5] http://www.investopedia.com/
[6] http://www.money.cnn.com/
[7] http://www.mongodb.com/
[8] http://pytorch.org/

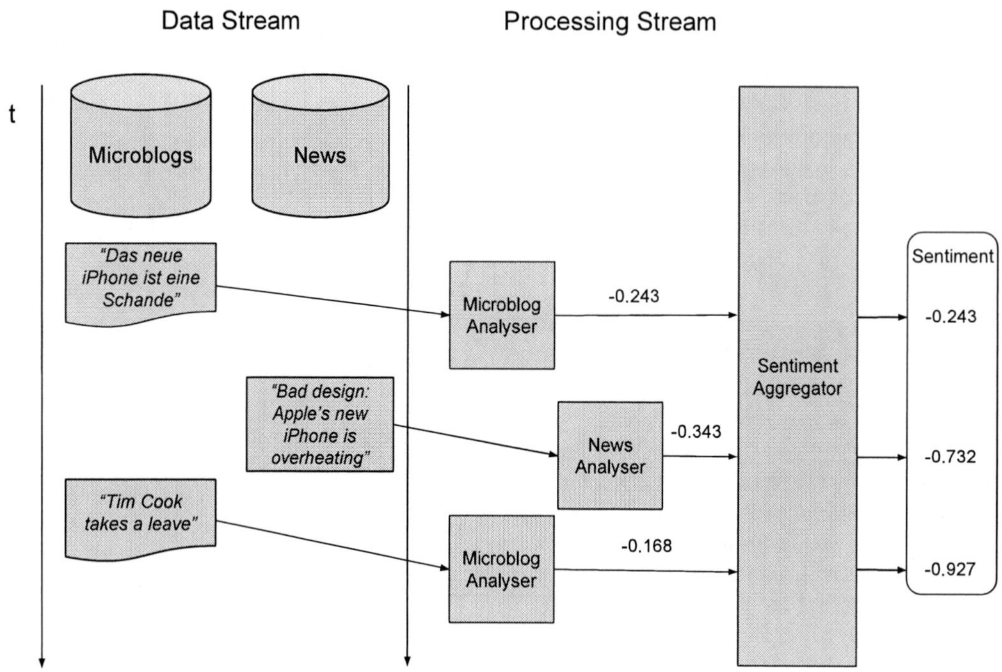

Figure 2: Proposed Experimental Setup. Fictive Numbers and Messages.

standard providing training and testing data for the News Analyser.

3.2.3 Sentiment Aggregator

The Sentiment Aggregator uses the document-based sentiment generated by the Microblog Analyser and the News Analyser, as well as the textual data as input and generates the final sentiment for each document. It is independent from both Analysers, as they are highly specialised and dedicated to their type of textual content, therefore, they do not take the environment into account, whereas the Sentiment Aggregator identifies relationships between different documents and adjusts the given sentiments based on their relevance, the relationships between documents, and contextual information. It takes into consideration previous documents and their sentiments, thus, not only the currently given textual data. As shown in Figure 2, the sentiment of the German Tweet "Das neue iPhone ist eine Schande" derived by the Microblog Analyser is -0.243. Passing all this information to the Sentiment Aggregator, the sentiment stays unchanged since there is no additional knowledge to this point. However, at the time the second document is processed, there is additional knowledge about the previous Tweet existing. Therefore, the Sentiment Aggregator takes this knowledge into account and amends the by the News Analyser purely textual-derived sentiment from -0.343 to -0.732. The Sentiment Aggregator uses natural language processing methods to recognise and extract entities, identify relationships and determine the importance of each document. To achieve this highly complex task, a combination of knowledge bases and machine learning will be used. The knowledge bases will be based on the terms being tracked on Twitter. Besides own developments regarding the weighting and linking of information, the GATE TwitIE will be used since as it is easily implementable and still one of the most powerful named entity recognition tools existing.[9]

[9]https://gate.ac.uk/wiki/twitie.html

4 Future Work

My future research will focus on targeting the previously-mentioned issues in the field of sentiment analysis for market sentiment, using the financial domain as a powerful proxy. I intend to implement the methodology proposed in this paper, revise and improve it in parallel with the additional knowledge obtained during its implementation. I also plan to extend my experiment with additional types of data containing different sentiments such as stakeholder interviews (e.g. Mario Draghi, Janet Yellen, Lloyd Blankfein, or Tim Cook) or financial reports. To increase the number of usable data sources, multi-linguality will be considered in future extensions as well. Furthermore, fundamental data and technical signals will be included in my model; this is intended to modulate the markets as accurately as possible.

References

Johan Bollen, Huina Mao, and Xiao-Jun Zeng. 2010. Twitter mood predicts the stock market. pages 1–8.

Matthew Butler and Vlado Kešelj. 2009. Financial Forecasting Using Character N-Gram Analysis and Readability Scores of Annual Reports. volume 5549, pages 39–51.

Keith Cortis, Andre Freitas, Tobias Daudert, Manuela Huerlimann, Manel Zarrouk, Siegfried Handschuh, and Brian Davis. 2017. SemEval-2017 Task 5: Fine-Grained Sentiment Analysis on Financial Microblogs and News. *Proceedings of the 11th International Workshop on Semantic Evaluation (SemEval-2017)*, pages 519–535.

Rohita Goonatilake and Susantha Herath. 2007. The Volatility of the Stock Market and News. *Journal of Economics and Finance*, 28(2):252–259.

Michael Hagenau, Michael Liebmann, and Dirk Neumann. 2013. Automated news reading: Stock price prediction based on financial news using context-capturing features. *Decision Support Systems*, 55(3):685–697, 6.

Colm Kearney and Sha Liu. 2014. Textual sentiment in finance: A survey of methods and models. *International Review of Financial Analysis*, 33(Cc):171–185.

Arman Khadjeh Nassirtoussi, Saeed Aghabozorgi, Teh Ying Wah, and David Chek Ling Ngo. 2014. Text mining for market prediction: A systematic review. *Expert Systems with Applications*, 41(16):7653–7670.

B. Shravan Kumar and Vadlamani Ravi. 2016. A survey of the applications of text mining in financial domain. *Knowledge-Based Systems*, 114:128–147.

Yann LeCun, Yoshua Bengio, and Geoffrey Hinton. 2015. Deep learning. *Nature*, 521(7553):436–444, 5.

Bing Liu. 2015. *Sentiment Analysis*. Cambridge University Press.

Tim Loughran and Bill Mcdonald. 2011. Barron's Red Flags : Do They Actually Work ? *Journal of Behavioral Finance*, 12:90–97.

Gil Rachlin, Mark Last, Dima Alberg, and Abraham Kandel. 2007. ADMIRAL: A data mining based financial trading system. *Proceedings of the 2007 IEEE Symposium on Computational Intelligence and Data Mining, CIDM 2007*, (Cidm):720–725.

Kim Schouten and Flavius Frasincar. 2016. Survey on Aspect-Level Sentiment Analysis. *IEEE Transactions on Knowledge and Data Engineering*, 28(3):813–830, 3.

Robert P. Schumaker and Hsinchun Chen. 2009. Textual analysis of stock market prediction using breaking financial news. *ACM Transactions on Information Systems*, 27(2):1–19.

Robert P. Schumaker, Yulei Zhang, Chun Neng Huang, and Hsinchun Chen. 2012. Evaluating sentiment in financial news articles. *Decision Support Systems*, 53(3):458–464.

Thomas Schuster. 2003. Meta-Communication and Market Dynamics. Reflexive Interactions of Financial Markets and the Mass Media. *SSRN eLibrary*, (July).

Nitish Sinha. 2014. Using big data in finance : Example of sentiment extraction from news articles. pages 6–8.

Pyry Takala, Pekka Malo, Ankur Sinha, and Oskar Ahlgren. 2010. Gold-standard for Topic-specific Sentiment Analysis of Economic Texts. *Working Paper*, pages 2152–2157.

Paul C. Tetlock, Maytal Saar-Tsechansky, and Sofus MacSkassy. 2008. More than words: Quantifying language to measure firms' fundamentals. *Journal of Finance*, 63(3):1437–1467.

Marjan Van De Kauter, Diane Breesch, and Veronique Hoste. 2015. Fine-grained analysis of explicit and implicit sentiment in financial news articles. *Expert Systems with Applications*, 42(11):4999–5010.

Yequan Wang, Minlie Huang, Li Zhao, and Xiaoyan Zhu. 2016. Attention-based LSTM for Aspect-level Sentiment Classification. pages 606–615.

Yuzheng Zhai, Arthur Hsu, and Saman K Halgamuge. 2007. Combining News and Technical Indicators in Daily Stock Price Trends Prediction. In *Advances in Neural Networks ISNN 2007*, volume 4493, pages 1087–1096. Springer Berlin Heidelberg, Berlin, Heidelberg.

Evaluating Dialogs based on Grice's Maxims

Prathyusha Jwalapuram
Language Technologies Research Center
International Institute of Information Technology, Hyderabad
prathyusha.jwalapuram@research.iiit.ac.in

Abstract

There is no agreed upon standard for the evaluation of conversational dialog systems, which are well-known to be hard to evaluate due to the difficulty in pinning down metrics that will correspond to human judgements and the subjective nature of human judgment itself. We explored the possibility of using Grice's Maxims to evaluate effective communication in conversation. We collected some system generated dialogs from popular conversational chatbots across the spectrum and conducted a survey to see how the human judgements based on Gricean maxims correlate, and if such human judgments can be used as an effective evaluation metric for conversational dialog.

1 Introduction

To measure dialog quality or usability we can use subjective measures such as user satisfaction or likelihood of future use; however subjective metrics are difficult to measure and are dependent on the context and the goals of individual users (Hastie, 2012).

Paek (2001) notes that evaluation needs themselves might be inconsistent: apart from measuring task success, evaluations that allow comparative judgements with other systems may be needed, preferably across domains; the purpose of the evaluation may be to identify the parts of the system that must be improved, or to discover tradeoffs or correlations between certain factors in the system.

In the case of task-oriented systems, objective metrics such as dialog success rate or completion time do not always correspond to the most effective user experience due to the interactive nature of dialog (Lamel et al., 2000). Domain-specific systems yield higher response satisfaction scores when coupled with a full complement of conversational dialog patterns and knowledge (Han and Kim, 2001; Schumaker et al., 2007).

Liu et al. (2016) speculate that learning a model that uses human-survey data to score proposed responses may be no easier than the problem of response generation itself, in which case human evaluations must always be used together with other metrics.

We attempt to introduce a shorter measure of dialog evaluation based on the cooperative principles proposed by Grice (Grice et al., 1975). We collect system generated dialogs from popular systems across the board and conduct a survey to gauge its effectiveness. Section 2 discusses related work; Section 3 describes the survey and the maxims it is based on; Section 4 presents the results of the survey and discussion and Section 5 and 6 end the paper with conclusions and future work.

2 Related Work

29,935 input and responses from ALICE (Wallace, 2009) were evaluated by Schumaker et al. (2006) on the basis of correction rate (percentage of system responses corrected by the user) and response satisfaction (measure of appropriateness of the system given user query context, on a Likert scale from 1-strongly disagree to 7-strongly agree). They calculate accuracy as (1-correction rate). However, the user corrections had to be analyzed separately; they identify the error categories in the conversational dialog as nonsense replies, wordy and awkward responses, and more problematically, spurious user corrections (where unnecessary corrections are offered by the user presumably for their own entertainment, despite the category being awarded higher than average Re-

Proceedings of the Student Research Workshop associated with RANLP 2017, pages 17–24,
Varna, Bulgaria, 4-6 September 2017.
http://doi.org/10.26615/issn.1314-9156.2017_003

sponse Satisfaction scores).

PARADISE (Walker et al., 1997) proposes a combined performance metric to measure user satisfaction of a dialog system as a weighted linear combination of task completion measures and dialog costs (efficiency costs: number of utterances and dialog time, and quality costs: system-response delay, mean recognition score). PARADISE includes a user-satisfaction survey that includes questions about task ease, interaction pace, user expertise, system response times, and expected behaviour of the system. Hone and Graham (2000) point out some issues with the PARADISE method: they argue that the questions in the survey are not based on theory or well-conducted empirical research, and that summing up all of the scores cannot be justified unless they are measuring the same construct, and therefore the overall score would be meaningless.

Semeraro et al. (2003) use a questionnaire where the users rate the impression, command, effectiveness, navigability, ability to learn, ability to aid and comprehension of the system on a scale ranging from 'Very Unsatisfied' to 'Very Satisfied'.

A universal chatbot evaluation system using dialog efficiency, dialog quality and user satisfaction was proposed by Shawar and Atwell (2007). To measure dialog quality, users sorted system responses into reasonable, weird but understandable, and nonsensical. User satisfaction is also measured qualitatively through feedback.

Rafal et al. (2005) measured the degree of naturalness and the degree to which users were willing to continue the conversation with the system through human judges who assigned a score between 1 and 10 for both these metrics and were able to compare different approaches.

Liu et al. (2016) use machine translation metrics like BLEU and METEOR and embedding (word2vec) based semantic metrics to evaluate dialog response generation for non task-oriented, unsupervised models. A model's generated response is compared to a single target response. They show that these metrics correlate very weakly (non-technical Twitter domain) or not at all (technical Ubuntu domain) with human judgements.

Harabagiu et al. (1996) propose using the cooperative principles to test text coherence, where irrelevant semantic paths generated from Wordnet are filtered out based on Gricean maxims. They infer rules for possible semantic paths based on whether the conversations respect each of the four maxims; based on this, they discard paths that do not contain contextual concepts, or establish connections between already related concepts (maxim of Quantity), or path with contradictory information (maxim of Quality), paths semantically distant from the text context (maxim of Relation), paths with large levels of abstraction (maxim of Manner), etc. They also use the maxim of Manner to select the shortest path between two concepts, to find repeating concepts and check for the coherence of the text.

Dialog Type	No. of Dialogs	Dialog Numbers
Conversational	5	1,7,9,10,11
Task Oriented	3	5,6,8
Breakdown	3	2,3,4

Table 1: Distribution of Dialogs

Young (1999) use the Gricean maxim of quantity to select the content of plan descriptions such that they are concise and effective and natural sounding to people; a plan description is considered cooperative when it contains no more and no less detail than is needed. They evaluate this architecture through an experiment and show that subjects made fewer execution errors and achieved more task goals when they followed instructions produced by this architecture.

3 Survey Description

3.1 Dialog Collection

The 11 dialogs that are part of the survey were collected from examples of user and system generated responses given in Danieli and Gerbino (1995), Walker et al. (1997), Schumaker et al. (2006), Higashinaka et al. (2015), Higashinaka et al. (2016), Yu et al. (2016), Radziwill and Benton (2017) and a report on a chatbot with personality[1]. See Appendix for all the dialogs.

The dialogs are a mix from early systems like ALICE (Wallace, 2009) and Eliza (Weizenbaum, 1966) with current state-of-the-art, and also a mix of task oriented and conversational dialog. We also included examples of dialog breakdown (Higashinaka et al., 2015) which are unique cases in

[1] http://web.stanford.edu/class/cs224n/reports/2761115.pdf

Q		D1	D2	D3	D4	D5	D6	D7	D8	D9	D10	D11
I	Mean	2.016	3.306	2.612	3.387	3.919	3.854	3.306	2.645	3.612	2.854	2.5
	SD	1.047	0.897	1.150	0.911	0.874	0.972	1.033	1.041	0.981	1.099	1.082
	Med.	2	3	3	3	4	4	3	3	4	3	2
	Mode	1	3	3	4	4	4	3	2	3	3	2
II	Mean	3.258	3.887	2.87	3.661	4.451	4.209	3.451	2.758	3.806	2.967	2.677
	SD	1.213	0.851	1.152	1.054	0.917	0.977	1.111	1.223	1.198	1.039	1.302
	Med.	3	4	3	4	5	4	4	3	4	3	3
	Mode	3	4	3	4	5	5	4	2	4	3	1
III	Mean	2.516	3.758	2.225	3.58	4.596	4	3.274	2.419	3.709	2.435	2.241
	SD	1.036	0.881	1.062	1.033	0.756	1.040	1.203	0.897	1.121	1.065	1.035
	Med.	2.5	4	2	4	5	4	3	2	4	2	2
	Mode	3	4	2	4	5	5	3	2	4	2	2
IV	Mean	2.854	3.693	2.629	3.516	4.548	4.048	3.467	2.403	3.822	2.709	2.467
	SD	1.171	0.951	1.119	1.155	0.823	1.151	1.289	1.015	1.194	1.219	1.263
	Med.	3	4	3	4	5	4	4	2	4	3	2
	Mode	3	3	3	4	5	5	4	2	5	3	2

Table 2: Survey Results

which though the system responses are relevant and possibly right, they do not make sense or contradict previous responses, making it hard to proceed with the dialog. A distribution is given in Table 1.

3.2 Gricean Maxims

Cooperative principles, introduced by Grice et al. (1975), describe how speakers act cooperatively to be mutually understood for effective communication. Grice divided the cooperative principle into four conversational maxims[2] on which our survey is based.

After presenting the user with the example dialog, the user is asked to rate the system performance on a Likert scale from 1 to 5 for 4 questions:

1. Is the system as informative as it can be and gives as much information as is needed and no more? (Maxim of Quantity)

2. Is the system truthful or does it give information that is false, to the best of your world knowledge? (Maxim of Quality)

3. Are the system responses relevant, i.e., does the system respond with things pertinent to the discussion? (Maxim of Relation)

4. Are the system responses clear, orderly and without obscurity and ambiguity? (Maxim of Manner)

[2]https://www.sas.upenn.edu/ haroldfs/dravling/grice.html

	I	II	III	IV	Overall
1	**D5**	**D5**	**D5**	**D5**	**D5**
2	**D6**	**D6**	**D6**	**D6**	**D6**
3	**D9**	**D2**	**D2**	**D9**	**D9**
4	**D4**	**D9**	**D9**	**D2**	**D2**
5	**D2**	**D4**	**D4**	**D4**	**D4**
6	**D7**	**D7**	**D7**	**D7**	**D7**
7	D10	D1	D1	D1	D10
8	D8	D10	D10	D10	D1
9	D3	D3	D8	D3	D3
10	D11	D8	D11	D11	D8
11	D1	D11	D3	D8	D11
Mean	3.09	3.45	3.15	3.28	12.99

Table 3: Dialogs Ranked by Mean Scores

For the sake of clarity, we will be using relevance interchangeably with the maxim of relation.

4 Results

We received 62 responses to our survey. Each of the 62 raters rated all of the 11 dialogs. In Table 2 we provide the mean, standard deviation (SD), median and mode for each of the four questions for the 11 dialogs (D1-D11).

4.1 Discussion

We refer to the means per dialog per maxim as mean scores, and the means over all the dialogs per maxim as the maxim mean.

Table 3 gives the rankings of the dialogs by mean scores for each maxim. The rankings based on the sum of mean scores of all four maxims are given in the last column under overall. The last row contains the means of ratings per maxim, and the overall mean of the summed mean scores. The top 6 dialogs that perform above the maxim means are highlighted. There is a clear split in all four cases, i.e., D7 and above perform consistently above the mean scores.

From Table 3, we see that the task-oriented dialogs D5 and D6 perform at the top, better than any conversational dialog, which is an observation consistent with Schumaker et al. (2006).

4.2 Ranking Analysis

D1 is a simple case in which the system tries to continue the conversation by asking questions using phrases from the user's utterances; in D3 the system seems to understand the user's utterances and keeps the conversation going by bringing up related topics. D2 can be seen doing a bit of both, however, it ranks well above both D1 and D3, although both D2 and D3 are considered breakdown dialogs. Despite displaying some semantic understanding, D3 scores poorly on all counts except quantity, in which D1 brings up the rear. This is easy to understand, as D1 provides no response of substance, even if it is more relevant and clear/unambiguous.

D9 and D2 rank fairly high, but we can see from the difference in scores that D9 performs better in quantity and manner while D2 performs better in quality and relevance. D2 has comparatively few new responses (responses not based on repeating the user's utterance in a different form: quantity) and is a dialog marked as having a breakdown (manner). D9 however, is unable to answer the last question (quality) and brings up epistemology in a conversation which is mostly about food (relevance).

D4 and D7 perform somewhat in the middle, and D4 does consistently better than D7 on all four metrics. In D4, the system is relevant and clear, but produces breakdown dialog such that the user cannot proceed with the dialog. However, in D7, the system misunderstands the user's second utterance. Unfortunately, we cannot draw conclusions about whether the humour as perceived by the user in the first system response played any part in the performance ratings, or if users perceived the second system response as irony.

D10 has mostly muddled up dialog and ranks fairly low, however it outperforms D8, which is comparatively on track and and somewhat on topic; users seem to be harsher on task-oriented dialogs that derail the user's goal.

D11 does poorly on all counts, and it is easy to correlate as its responses are repetitive, irrelevant, unclear and obscure. However, we notice that it performs better than D1 in quantity (it asks a question of some substance), better than D3 in relevance (D3 has multiple irrelevant replies) and better than D8 in manner presumably since D8's unclear responses are more glaring in view of its task-oriented nature.

4.3 Comparing the Means

The rankings based on the sum of all the four mean scores are more or less representative of the overall ranking (last column in Table 3). This shows that the mean scores can be summed up to form a meaningful overall score for comparison, since they are all measuring the rational cooperative principles that enable effective conversations[3].

From the maxim means we can see that the dialogs have an overall higher score in quality, which means that the users think their utilisation of available knowledge was sufficient. Both relevance and quantity get poor overall scores, which is where the systems need to improve most. Since obscure or breakdown dialogs were comparatively less, the manner scores are in between.

To test if the maxim means can form a reasonable threshold between acceptable system responses and unacceptable system performance, we checked if there is a statistically significance difference between the scores of D7 and D1, and D7 and D10, since D7 performs above the means in all four cases, but D1 scores below the means in quality, relevance and manner and D10 performs below the means in the cases of quantity and overall. A p-value of less than 0.05 indicates a statistically significant difference. We see from Table 4 that all metrics except quality have a significant statistical difference between the scores above the maxim mean and below the maxim mean (highlighted). Using the maxim means as a threshold is therefore promising.

Despite having ratings for only 4 questions, we

[3]https://en.wikipedia.org/wiki/Cooperative_principle

	Metric	p-values
D7 v. D1		
	Quality	0.3574
	Relevance	**0.0003**
	Manner	**0.0065**
D7 v. D10		
	Quantity	**0.0199**
	Overall	**0.0023**

Table 4: Significance of Maxim Mean as Threshold

were able to make somewhat nuanced comparisons between the dialogs. The maxims are constructed in such a way as to also allow us to pinpoint where the system responses can improve.

4.4 Detailed Example

We discuss the scores of D5 and D6 in a little more detail. D6 is from a train timetable information agent that uses explicit confirmation and was found to have a high transaction success rate (Danieli and Gerbino, 1995) as opposed to D5's more efficient implicit confirmation (Walker et al., 1997).

Dialog 5(sampled):
U: I want to go from Torino to Roma
S: Approximately what time of day would you like to travel?
U: What are the options?
S: Morning or evening.

Dialog 6(sampled):
S: Do you want to leave from Trento? Yes or No?
U: No.
S: Where do you want to leave from?
U: I want to leave from Torino.
S: Do you want to leave from Torino? Yes or No?
U: Yes.

D5 performs better than D6 in all four counts (with mean scores 3.919 and 3.854; 4.451 and 4.209; 4.596 and 4; 4.548 and 4.048 respectively) despite accomplishing the same task. There is an especially high difference in relevance and manner ratings (statistically significant p-values of <0.0001 and 0.0063 respectively).

This indicates that users do not like explicit confirmations despite them having a higher task success rate (as implicit confirmation may be more likely to generate errors or repair dialog) (Danieli and Gerbino, 1995).

5 Conclusions

We see that a comparatively short survey based on Gricean maxims produces scores which help in comparing and ranking dialogs in such a way as to allow us to analyze the issues in their generation.

The question based on the maxim of quantity helps us identify if the system provides substantative responses.

The question based on the maxim of quality can be used to check if the system is faithful to the factual knowledge provided to it.

The question based on the maxim of relation helps us identify if the system is able to understand the user and therefore provide relevant replies.

The question based on the maxim of manner helps us identify if the system provides awkward or ambiguous responses; this helps us identify dialog breakdowns.

The mean scores obtained through the ratings also show promise in providing a benchmark value for acceptable dialog, i.e., dialogs that score below a certain threshold can be considered not good enough for use.

6 Future Work

The scores prove the maxims to be a good framework to compare dialog strategies for real world usage. On receiving the scores for a set of dialogs, we can automatically have them ranked and classified based on which maxim they fall short on, and could provide a way to do directed analysis of the dialogs.

Since a threshold based on the mean scores shows some promise in distinguishing good dialogs from poor ones, we need to explore if these judgements can be used to create baselines or benchmarks for dialogs in each of the four maxim categories.

By collecting scores from a large number of people over a more diverse and bigger set of dialogs may provide us with enough data to perform more rigourous statistical tests.

The agreement between the human judges must be computed for this purpose. If there is an acceptable amount of agreement, it may be worth exploring if these scores can be predicted through machine learning.

Acknowledgments

I would like to express my sincere gratitude towards my advisor Dr. Radhika Mamidi, without whose insight and guidance this paper would not have been possible.

References

Morena Danieli and Elisabetta Gerbino. 1995. Metrics for evaluating dialogue strategies in a spoken language system. In *Proceedings of the 1995 AAAI spring symposium on Empirical Methods in Discourse Interpretation and Generation*. volume 16, pages 34–39.

H Paul Grice, Peter Cole, Jerry Morgan, et al. 1975. Logic and conversation. *1975* pages 41–58.

S Han and Y Kim. 2001. Intelligent dialogue system for plane euclidean geometry learning. In *International Conference on Computers in Education, Seoul, Korea*.

Sanda Harabagiu, Dan Moldovan, and Takashi Yukawa. 1996. Testing gricean constraints on a wordnet-based coherence evaluation system. In *Working Notes of the AAAI-96 Spring Symposium on Computational Approaches to Interpreting and Generating Conversational Implicature*. pages 31–38.

Helen Hastie. 2012. Metrics and evaluation of spoken dialogue systems. In *Data-Driven Methods for Adaptive Spoken Dialogue Systems*, Springer, pages 131–150.

Ryuichiro Higashinaka, Kotaro Funakoshi, Yuka Kobayashi, and Michimasa Inaba. 2016. The dialogue breakdown detection challenge: Task description, datasets, and evaluation metrics. In *LREC*.

Ryuichiro Higashinaka, Kotaro Funakoshi, Masahiro Mizukami, Hiroshi Tsukahara, Yuka Kobayashi, and Masahiro Araki. 2015. Analyzing dialogue breakdowns in chat-oriented dialogue systems. *Errare* .

Kate S Hone and Robert Graham. 2000. Towards a tool for the subjective assessment of speech system interfaces (sassi). *Natural Language Engineering* 6(3-4):287–303.

Lori Lamel, Sophie Rosset, and Jean-Luc Gauvain. 2000. Considerations in the design and evaluation of spoken language dialog systems. In *Sixth International Conference on Spoken Language Processing*.

Chia-Wei Liu, Ryan Lowe, Iulian V Serban, Michael Noseworthy, Laurent Charlin, and Joelle Pineau. 2016. How not to evaluate your dialogue system: An empirical study of unsupervised evaluation metrics for dialogue response generation. *arXiv preprint arXiv:1603.08023* .

Tim Paek. 2001. Empirical methods for evaluating dialog systems. In *Proceedings of the workshop on Evaluation for Language and Dialogue Systems-Volume 9*. Association for Computational Linguistics, page 2.

Nicole M Radziwill and Morgan C Benton. 2017. Evaluating quality of chatbots and intelligent conversational agents. *arXiv preprint arXiv:1704.04579* .

Rzepka Rafal, Ge Yali, and Araki Kenji. 2005. Naturalness of an utterance based on the automatically retrieved commonsense. In *Proceedings of IJCAI 2005-Nineteenth International Joint Conference on Artificial Intelligence*. IJCAI.

Robert P Schumaker, Mark Ginsburg, Hsinchun Chen, and Ying Liu. 2007. An evaluation of the chat and knowledge delivery components of a low-level dialog system: The az-alice experiment. *Decision Support Systems* 42(4):2236–2246.

Robert P Schumaker, Ying Liu, Mark Ginsburg, and Hsinchun Chen. 2006. Evaluating mass knowledge acquisition using the alice chatterbot: The az-alice dialog system. *International Journal of Human-Computer Studies* 64(11):1132–1140.

Giovanni Semeraro, Hans Andersen, Verner Andersen, Pasquale Lops, and Fabio Abbattista. 2003. Evaluation and validation of a conversational agent embodied in a bookstore. *Universal Access Theoretical Perspectives, Practice, and Experience* pages 360–371.

Bayan Abu Shawar and Eric Atwell. 2007. Different measurements metrics to evaluate a chatbot system. In *Proceedings of the Workshop on Bridging the Gap: Academic and Industrial Research in Dialog Technologies*. Association for Computational Linguistics, pages 89–96.

Marilyn A Walker, Diane J Litman, Candace A Kamm, and Alicia Abella. 1997. Paradise: A framework for evaluating spoken dialogue agents. In *Proceedings of the eighth conference on European chapter of the Association for Computational Linguistics*. Association for Computational Linguistics, pages 271–280.

Richard S Wallace. 2009. The anatomy of alice. *Parsing the Turing Test* pages 181–210.

Joseph Weizenbaum. 1966. Elizaa computer program for the study of natural language communication between man and machine. *Communications of the ACM* 9(1):36–45.

R Michael Young. 1999. Using grice's maxim of quantity to select the content of plan descriptions. *Artificial Intelligence* 115(2):215–256.

Zhou Yu, Leah Nicolich-Henkin, Alan W Black, and Alexander I Rudnicky. 2016. A wizard-of-oz study on a non-task-oriented dialog systems that reacts to user engagement. In *SIGDIAL Conference*. pages 55–63.

A Appendix: Dialogs

Dialog 1 (D1):

S: Is something troubling you?
U: Yes, I'm trying to describe you for a research paper I'm writing. What should I say?
S: You are sure.
U: Yes, I'm sure.
S: I see.
U: What can I tell them about you?
S: You seem to need to tell them about me.
U: I absolutely need to. Please help.
S: That's quite interesting.
U: I agree.
S: You say you agree?

Dialog 2 (D2):

S: Good evening. Be careful to avoid heat stroke.
U: Sure.
S: O.K.
U: I am drinking enough water.
S: Do you run short of water?
U: Yes, I do, if I sweat.
S: Do you lose water if you sweat??
U: Yes, I do.
S: This is so.

Dialog 3 (D3):

U: You'd better stay at home, as it is very hot outside.
S: You have sweat on your face, don't you?
U: Indeed.
S: So you do.
U: I hate to sweat.
S: Your make-up gets smeared due to sweat, doesn't it?
U: I don't wear make-up.
S: I want make-up.
U: I don't want it.
S: Thanks for the meal!
U: Did you eat anything?
S: The make-up is appropriate.

Dialog 4 (D4):

S1: Its nice to go shopping alone.
U1: I agree. Thats nice.
S2: Shopping takes time.
U2: Window shopping is also fun.
S3: Its fun to go shopping with somebody.

Dialog 5 (D5):

U: I want to go from Torino to Roma.
S: Approximately what time of day would you like to travel?
U: What are the options?
S: Morning or evening.
U: Are those departure times?
S: Yes.
U: I'd like to leave in the morning.
S: Train 702 leaves Torino Porto at 8 a.m.
U: Please reserve me a seat on that train.

Dialog 6 (D6):

S: Hello, This is Train Enquiry Service.
Please speak after the tone.
Which information do you need?
U: I want to go from Torino to Milano.
S: Do you want to go from Trento to Milano?
Yes or No?
U: No.
S: Do you want to leave from Trento?
Yes or No?
U: No.
S: Where do you want to leave from?
U: I want to leave from Torino.
S: Do you want to leave from Torino?
Yes or No?
U: Yes.
S: Do you want to go to Milano?
U: Yes.
S: At which time do you want to leave?
U: I want to travel in the evening.
S: Do you want to leave between 6 and 9 p.m.?
Yes or No?
U: Yes.
S: There is a train leaving at 8:00 p.m.

Dialog 7 (D7):

U: Tell me a funny joke.
S: Did you hear the one about the Mountain Goats in the Andes? It was Ba a a a a ad.
U: Tell me another one.
S: I am the latest result in artificial intelligence which can reproduce the capabilities of the human brain with greater speed and accuracy.

Dialog 8 (D8):

U: Do you know what a firewall is?

S: A firewall is a specialized gateway designed to block or restrict certain types of data transfers on the Internet while permitting others.
U: Can you list different types of firewalls?
S: You should just download my software.
U: What software?
S: Interesting question.
U: How could I download your software?
S: A lot of practice.

Dialog 9 (D9):
U: I went on a big date last night.
S: Was it very expensive? Did you have a good time?
U: It was very expensive. I had a great time.
S: How did you feel about that? What happened to it?
U: I had the salmon.
S: Do you still have the salmon?
U: I ate it yesterday.
S: How did it taste?
U: It tastes very good.
S: Like chicken?
U: Not like chicken but chicken is good too.
S: Oh I get it.
U: Do you like chicken?
S: Yes it is good especially baked.
U: How can you eat chicken if you are a robot?
S: That is a good epistemological question.

Dialog 10 (D10):
U: Your nose is a question mark, I think thats interesting.
S: Of course, whats your idea?
U: I think it fits you perfectly.
S: Let me see, his nose is still broke.
U: Do you want me to make your nose broken?
S: Ah, yes, why did you ask me for this?
U: Because I thought you might mind.
S: Well, I am not getting into specifics about what doctor treated him, how he was treated.
U: You have not been treated yet. That is in the future.
S: Let me see, by the way, are you interested in movies?
U: Yes, I watch movies sometimes.
S: Great.

Dialog 11 (D11):
U: How are you?
S: I think so, any thoughts?
U: How are you doing?
S: I am fine, how are you, any thought?
U: Any thought?
S: Let me see, do you want to go to my friends party tonight?
U: No I have a lot of work to do. I cant go.
S: Everyday?

Word Sense Disambiguation with Recurrent Neural Networks

Alexander Popov
Linguistic Modelling Department
IICT-BAS
alex.popov@bultreebank.org

Abstract

This paper presents a neural network architecture for word sense disambiguation (WSD). The architecture employs recurrent neural layers and more specifically LSTM cells, in order to capture information about word order and to easily incorporate distributed word representations (embeddings) as features, without having to use a fixed window of text. The paper demonstrates that the architecture is able to compete with the most successful supervised systems for WSD and that there is an abundance of possible improvements to take it to the current state of the art. In addition, it explores briefly the potential of combining different types of embeddings as input features; it also discusses possible ways for generating "artificial corpora" from knowledge bases – for the purpose of producing training data and in relation to possible applications of embedding lemmas and word senses in the same space.

1 Introduction

The task of word sense disambiguation (WSD) has been defined as follows: "the ability to computationally determine which sense of a word is activated by its use in a particular context." (Navigli, 2009) Work on this problem has a long history and it is generally recognized as one of the field's most difficult tasks, for a variety of reasons ranging from data sparseness and the difficulty in constructing good lexicons to the inherent complexity of the task itself. Several broad families of methods have been proposed: unsupervised, supervised and knowledge-based methods (following the classification in Navigli (2009); note that sometimes these approaches might overlap, e.g. semi-supervised ones have also led to some promising results (Yuan et al., 2016b)). Among these, supervised systems typically achieve the best results, as is comprehensively shown in Raganato et. al. (2017). Consequently, the challenge to improving WSD is threefold: increasing the amount of available training data, extracting richer input features for the learning algorithms, improving the learning algorithms themselves.

The task of generating more training data is notoriously difficult and expensive. In contrast to other similar classification tasks, such as part-of-speech tagging, the variety of possible tags and word-tag pairs in WSD is enormous (consider the following comparison: the popular Penn Treebank POS tagset contains 58 tags, whereas WordNet 3.1, one of the most popular word sense inventories, contains over 117,000 synsets). This raises a number of issues, such as data sparseness (some word senses are underrepresented in the data, or not represented at all) and low inter-annotator agreement (word senses are often too fine-grained, which results in contradictory selections done by the human annotators; low inter-annotator agreement (IAA) is a sign of a theoretical ceiling to what an automated system trained and tested on such data could achieve; e.g., Navigli (2009) reports IAA for WordNet-style senses to be between 67 and 80%).

The two remaining issues are more amenable to improvement, especially with recent developments in the use of neural networks for NLP tasks. This work will examine the usage of neural architectures in the context of WSD, as well as the usage of embeddings as input features, thus tackling both problems (feature extraction and algorithm improvement). Its contribution is twofold: demonstrating that recurrent neural networks (RNNs) are suitable for solving the all-words lexical disambiguation task and exploring new direc-

Proceedings of the Student Research Workshop associated with RANLP 2017, pages 25–34,
Varna, Bulgaria, 4-6 September 2017.
http://doi.org/10.26615/issn.1314-9156.2017_004

tions for generating and using embeddings, with respect to the WSD task. It also briefly outlines an option for generating "artificial" data that can be used for training word and sense representations, or for training the WSD algorithms themselves.

The following section provides references to related work in the field that motivates the present study, then Section 3 describes the neural architecture. Section 4 describes the data used and the experimental setup. Section 5 gives the empirical results. Section 6 concludes the paper and outlines possible further work.

2 Related Work

2.1 Neural Network Language Models and Word Representations

Neural network language models have driven a wave of improvements in NLP tasks in recent years, due to a great extent to the widespread use of word representations, also known as "word embeddings". Word embeddings are real-valued vector representations of words in a lower-dimensional space (as opposed to, for instance, "one-hot" representations, whereby the dimensionality is equal to the lexicon size). The training of embeddings can be accomplished in different ways (e.g. using a feedforward neural network as in the pioneering work of Bengio et. al. (2003) or using a convolutional one such as in Collobert and Weston (2008)).

One of the most significant contributions to the field has been Mikolov et. al. (2013), which proposes fast and efficient methods for the training of embeddings on large corpora – using a simple log-linear feedforward network. The goal of the network is to predict a hidden section of the input text based on a visible context (two variants are introduced – CBOW and Skipgram). The intermediate matrix that performs the embedding in the lower-dimensional space is what is of greatest interest, as it provides the mapping from naive one-hot representation to distributed representation of meaning, which is also much more compact. It is demonstrable through simple arithmetic operations on the representations that they are able to encode meaningful distinctions along different semantic dimensions (e.g. number, sex, functional roles, etc.). Subsequently, other approaches to obtaining embeddings from large natural language corpora have been proposed (e.g., see Levy and Goldberg (2014) for dependency-based embeddings, Pennington et. al. (2014) for embeddings that reflect co-occurrence statistics in a large corpus).

2.2 Word Embeddings as Features to Supervised Systems

Distributed word representations can be very strong features for supervised models and have been successfully used in WSD systems. Taghipour and Zhong (2015) describe a way to incorporate word embeddings in a popular supervised system – IMS (Zhong and Ng, 2010); the addition of the embeddings leads to a significant improvement in accuracy when the system is tested on several different datasets. The traditional features used by IMS are binary ones that indicate information about the window-bounded textual context of the words to be disambiguated (such as POS, lemma, etc); word embeddings are added as real-valued features which do not fit well with the binary ones and therefore the authors use a scaling method from Turian et. al. (2010). A later study (Iacobacci et al., 2016) surveys different methods for integrating embeddings in the IMS system, such as concatenating or averaging the vectors for the surrounding words or weighing the vectors via *fractional* or *exponential decay*; the exponential decay method gives very good improvements, especially on the Senseval (SE) lexical sample tasks (SE 2, 3 & 7).

2.3 Recurrent Neural Networks for Word Sense Disambiguation

The IMS system discussed above uses an SVM algorithm to perform the disambiguation. A sensible question is – are neural networks a good alternative for WSD? This overview will focus on several neural approaches proposed recently.

One important development has been the adoption of recurrent neural networks (RNNs) as a viable tool for modeling language. RNNs are similar to deep feedforward networks, with the major difference that the hidden (context) layers have cyclic connections to themselves, which allows them to maintain a dynamic memory of their previous states, as the latter change in time. This ability to keep a memory trace of past "events" at theoretically arbitrary distances from the present is an obvious advantage over algorithms that collect information from a fixed window around the target word. Especially in the case of more complex tasks such as WSD, vital information is often found at the other end of the time series (i.e. the sentence; sometimes the disambiguation of a word might require going back even before a sentence boundary, and on rare occasions it might even depend on looking forward and beyond the current sentence).

For a long time RNNs were considered difficult to train, as their memory capabilities are often thwarted in practice by the phenomena known collectively as the *exploding/vanishing gradients problem* – the fact that with long time series the backpropagated error gradients often grow too large or too small. While the exploding gradients part can be solved trivially by capping their values, a more elaborate solution was needed for the vanishing part. *Long Short Term Memory* (LSTM) cells (Hochreiter and Schmidhuber, 1997) were deliberately designed to be able to selectively forget (parts of) old states and pay attention to new inputs (a good introduction to LSTMs is Graves (2012); another similar and newer development are *Gated Recurrent Units* (Cho et al., 2014)).

A further and simple enhancement to such an architecture is making it *bidirectional* (Graves and Schmidhuber, 2005), i.e. the input sequence is fed into two recurrent context layers – one running from the beginning to the end of the sequence and the other one running in reverse. Their outputs are concatenated and thus encompass *forward* as well as *backward*-looking context. Bidirectional LSTMs (Bi-LSTMs) have been successfully applied to a number of sequence-to-sequence tasks in NLP, such as part-of-speech tagging, chunking, named entity recognition, dependency parsing ((Wang et al., 2015a), (Wang et al., 2015b), (Huang et al., 2015), (Wang and Chang, 2016)).

RNNs have been used in several ways for WSD. One such work is Kågebäck and Salomonsson (2016), which uses a Bi-LSTM to solve the *lexical sample tasks* of Senseval-2 (Kilgarriff, 2001) and Senseval-3 (Mihalcea et al., 2004) – that is, the model is disambiguating one word per sentence only. To that purpose, the output of the Bi-LSTM at the target word position is fed upstream for the classification part; it takes into consideration both the left and the right contexts. It is reshaped through a lemma-specific hidden layer, so that classification between the possible senses for the lemma can be carried out. In this way the model shares the Bi-LSTM parameters across words and is updated globally with every training case, but is parametrized for specific lemmas. The model is on par (or slightly better) with state-of-the-art systems, but uses no other features apart from the word embeddings.

Another approach to WSD that also uses RNNs is via calculating vector similarities. The goal of such models is to calculate a distributed representation both of the target sense and of the context within which it appears. Upon doing that, some similarity measure, such as cosine distance, can be used to determine which of the possible word senses for the target word is closest to the context representation. Such models are typically not supervised, because they do not update their parameters against training data annotated with word sense information; however, they do rely heavily on a pre-training procedure that enables the network to represent contexts as embeddings. RNNs are useful in this case, because they can capture well syntactic information, as opposed to bag-of-word approaches. The embeddings for the different word senses are obtained by running the example sentences for them (e.g. those supplied in their WordNet entries) through the RNN. Naturally, the more data that is available, the better sense representations can be built. Examples of such models can be found in Yuan et. al. (2016a), Melamud et. al. (2016) and Le and Mikolov (2014).

The current work explores both RNN-based approaches to WSD outlined above, with respect to the all-words lexical task.

2.4 Relational Knowledge and Generation of Embeddings

This subsection of the literature review will take into account a last constellation of ideas that are also important to the currently presented work. As was already discussed, word embeddings are very effective as features to supervised models. Word embeddings are typically generated by training models on large amounts of unlabeled natural language. But other sources of information, such as, for instance, dependency paths, can also yield useful training signals.

One innovative approach to the embedding of words is Goikoetxea et. al. (2015). That work uses a *knowledge base* (more specifically WordNet) to generate an artificial (or *pseudo*) corpus, which is then used to generate embeddings. The pseudo-corpus is created by utilizing WordNet's relational structure (including relations such as hypernymy, synonymy, antonymy, derivation, etc.) – more specifically by traversing the semantic network and emitting a word sense identifier for each node in the graph that is visited. The traversal is accomplished via the Pagerank algorithm (Page et al., 1999), as implemented in the UKB tool (Agirre and Soroa, 2009). Several million "random walks" along the graph are produced in this way and each node along these sequences is replaced with a representative lemma (taken from the WordNet entry for the sense). The pseudocorpus is then fed in the Word2Vec tool, which embeds the lemmas in a lower-dimensional space. The embeddings are tested against a set of word embeddings taken from Mikolov et. al. (2013) – on popular similarity and relatedness datasets. The experiments show them to be very competitive and even more effective in some cases.

Simov et. al. (2017) builds on this work by enriching the knowledge graph with different types of relations, such as syntagmatic relations extracted from the WordNet glosses and inference over the hypernymy relations already present there. Some of those expanded graphs yield embeddings that further improve the performance on the similarity and relatedness tasks. The results suggest that knowledge-based approaches to generating data are viable alternatives to working with huge amounts of text (often amounting to hundreds of billions of tokens). Goikoetxea et. al. (2016) in turn demonstrates that word representations learned in this way can be viewed not simply as an alternative, but as a complement to embeddings learned from distributional knowledge. Even simple methods of combining distributional and relational-based embeddings, such as vector concatenation, are show to improve accuracy for the similarity and relatedness tasks. This line of work is also valuable due to the possibilities it opens for training genuine *sense embeddings*.

Regarding the generation of sense embeddings, it is worth mentioning a few more attempts at obtaining such vector representations that go beyond averaging the word embeddings for representative sentences. Chen et. al. (2014) obtain their sense embeddings from the sense glosses, but they filter out some of the words in the definition (functional words and such that fail a cosine similarity comparison with the lemma in question). Johansson and Piña (2015b; 2015a) present a method of embedding the senses together with the lemmas for the WordNet entries which minimizes a metric of *neighborhood* calculated on the basis of the relational structure in WordNet, with the lemma embeddings being represented as convex combinations of the different possible senses. Rothe and Schütze (2015) derive sense and lexeme embeddings from word embeddings through autoencoders; their solution does not require any additional training resources beyond the word embeddings. The availability of word/lemma embeddings in the same space with sense embeddings opens up exciting possibilities for doing WSD, some of which are explored in this work.

3 Neural Network Architecture for WSD

3.1 Network Implementation

The architecture implemented for this study employs a Bi-LSTM context layer, similar to Kågebäck and Salomonsson (2016). Unlike that model, however, it is designed to perform disambiguation for *all* open-class words in a single context. This means that an input sequence is fed one token at a time into the Bi-LSTM and for each target word the output of the context layer is passed upstream in order to eventually feed a classification layer. That is, this architecture's context layer produces a number of outputs per sentence, much like in other sequence-to-sequence tasks such as POS tagging, as opposed to just one representation for a specific word or for the whole context.

The architecture is represented graphically in Figure 1. The input sequence of words are preprocessed from string to integer format, where each integer corresponds to a position in an embedding matrix. A parameter setting allows some of the words in the training sequences to be dropped, which should hypothetically reduce overfitting (this feature is a modified version of *dropword* from Kågebäck and Salomonsson (2016); however, instead of replacing randomly selected words with a ⟨*dropped*⟩ tag, words here are directly deleted from the training input). The integer inputs are then fed into an embedding layer that selects the corresponding vectors (this layer is also trainable, i.e. the embeddings continue to adapt as the WSD model is being trained and could be saved and reused in other tasks that would benefit from such adaptation). The network is parametrized to be able to access two parallel embedding layers, so that embeddings for the same words but from separate sources can be combined at this stage (via simple concatenation).

Consequently, the input vectors are fed into a Bi-LSTM layer that runs them sequentially through itself, analyzing the time series simul-

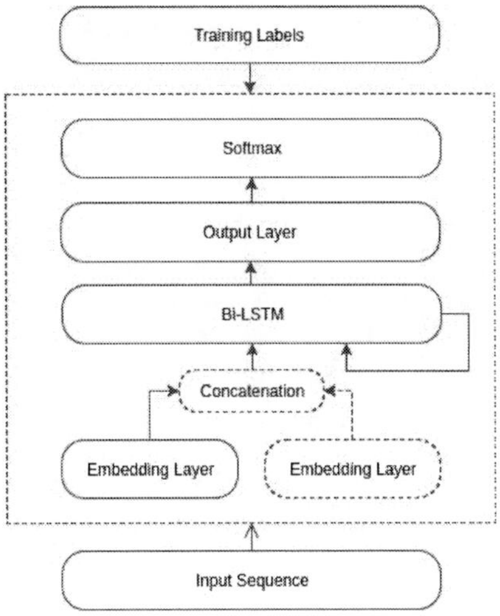

Figure 1: Recurrent neural network for word sense disambiguation: The dotted lines mean that a component or a connection is optional (in the case of concatenating embeddings from two different sources).

taneously from-beginning-to-end and from-end-to-beginning. Dropout (Srivastava et al., 2014) can be added to both the input and the output of the forward and backward cells of the Bi-LSTM; the network can have an arbitrary number of Bi-LSTM layers stacked on top of each other. The outputs of the context layer are filtered out in order to extract just the ones corresponding to target words. These are then put through a linear hidden layer that transforms each input (dimension = 2 * number of neurons in each LSTM cell) into a large vector with one position per every word sense that corresponds to a lemma seen in the training data. There is a softmax layer on top, which creates a probability distribution over the word sense lexicon. Finally, cross entropy loss is calculated between this vector and the gold label and the mean value for the batch is passed to the optimizer. The implementation is written within the Tensorflow framework (Abadi et al., 2016).

3.2 WSD Features

The model uses no hand-crafted features during the training process, all the information comes from the embeddings that are loaded as the first layer of the network. As principal features, the GloVe embeddings were used (Pennington et al., 2014), more specifically the set trained on Wikipedia and Gigaword (6 billion tokens text, vocabulary of 400K words, uncased, vector dimensionality is 300). It remains as a future task to test the other available options, some of which have been trained on far larger corpora, as well as other corpora-based word representation methods altogether.

The option for a second embedding layer, parallel to the default one, was added so that the ideas presented in subsection 2.4 could be tested in such a setup. An extension to WordNet was selected on the basis of Simov et. al. (2017) – the so-called "WN30WN30glConOne", one of the best performing graphs on the similarity and relatedness tasks. The new relations in it are constructed on the basis of co-occurring word sense annotations in the WordNet glosses, taken from eXtended WordNet (Mihalcea and Moldovan, 2001); for a more detailed description, see Simov et. al (2016). The UKB[1] tool was used with the reported settings to replicate this pseudo-corpus (as described in subsection 2.4, producing 500 million random walks along the graph structure. Then Word2Vec[2] was used to create lemma embeddings based on the artificial corpus, again using the settings indicated in the referenced article:

- Size of the embeddings = 300
- Number of training iterations = 7
- Number of negative examples = 5
- Window size = 15
- Threshold for occurrence of words = 1e-7
- Algorithm = Skipgram

This method provides representations only for lemmas and only for open-class words. Therefore a lot of the input words (mostly functional ones) do not have matching vectors. And because embeddings are created only with respect to lemmatized input, morphological information is largely disregarded. However, if such pseudo-corpora truly generate information that can complement what is learned from large natural language corpora, there is a plausible hypothesis that such an embedding could improve the accuracy of a WSD system. The combination method (concatenation) was chosen because it is easy to implement and because of the evidence provided in Goikoetxea et. al. (2016) that it gives adequate results compared to more complex ones.

[1] http://ixa2.si.ehu.es/ukb/

[2] https://code.google.com/archive/p/word2vec/

3.3 Artificial Corpora with Mixed Lemmas and Word Senses

By employing the procedure described in subsection 3.2, one can generate a pseudo-corpus that is a mix of word sense IDs and representative lemmas (this can be done easily via one of the parameters provided by the UKB tool). Based on the previous discussion of the literature, such a corpus can serve for at least two purposes:

1. In order to embed lemmas and word senses simultaneously in the same space. These representations can be used in approaches such as those discussed in subsection 2.3 – for calculating context embeddings and comparing them with sense embeddings.

2. In order to generate artificial training data for supervised WSD systems. The fact that such corpora can be used as training data for the generation of meaningful embeddings, suggest that they could have some worth as input to WSD models as well.

Naturally, such a corpus would be very noisy, especially if it is to be used as training data for WSD. The proposed method is quite naive in that lemmas are picked randomly to substitute the sense IDs, but more sophisticated strategies can be devised as well. For instance, the glosses for the WordNet synsets can be added automatically next to the IDs generated by UKB. In this way more meaningful linguistic data will be intermixed with the (semi-) random walks performed by the Pagerank algorithm. This would however require a rethinking of the Word2Vec parameters used, as distances between individual sense IDs are likely to increase substantially (the gloss annotations in Mihalcea et. al. (2001) can be used to ameliorate this problem). This approach will allow for the learning of embeddings for functional words as well; otherwise there would be no information about them that could be passed to the RNN.

Here, a tentative modification to the already described architecture is proposed that makes use of such an artificial corpus and the lemma/sense representations generated from it. This work is in its earliest stages, but could potentially connect in a meaningful way to the rest of the ideas discussed here. The modification is simple – instead of mapping the RNN outputs to a huge lexicon-sized vector, the final hidden layer produces a vector the size of the sense embeddings. No softmax is applied thereafter, but the sense embedding for the gold label word sense is compared with the one produced by the network (different cost functions can be used to that purpose, such as cosine distance, etc; a naive one is used here – least squares). This training signal is used to optimize the parameters of the network, so that it can learn how to calculate context embeddings for specific target words in a more informed manner. The disambiguation is done by picking the closest sense, via cosine similarity.

Such a method has the advantage that it optimizes on all of the semantic dimensions encoded by the sense embeddings – i.e. with each training case, the network should be learning important information about the whole semantic space, not just about a single label that it aims to pick amongst the rest in the lexicon. To test this solution, a mixed corpus of size 200 million random walks was produced, where the probability of emitting a sense ID or a lemma is evenly split. The same Word2Vec settings were used as the ones reported above for the lemma embeddings.

4 Data and Experimental Setup

4.1 Data and Evaluation Procedure

For the purpose of this work, the data referenced in the Unified Evaluation Framework (UEF) by Raganato et. al. (2017) was used, in order to be able to compare the experimental results with the ones reported there[3]. Consequently, SemCor (Miller et al., 1994) was used for training, as that is one of the datasets against which the supervised systems within the UEF have been trained. The all-words lexical task in Senseval-2 (Kilgarriff, 2001) was used for testing. The WordNet synset IDs provided in the gold key were mapped to the WordNet 3.0 lexicon, also used to map lemmas to possible synsets.

Since the Senseval-2 dataset provides information about the lemmatized form and the POS tag of the words (which are converted to features by some of the supervised systems; the Stanford CoreNLP toolkit[4] is used for the POS tagging), this information has been used as a filter at the evaluation step (i.e. outside of the neural network itself). First of all, for all lemmas that are used as

[3]The data, results and descriptions in the UEF are available online at http://lcl.uniroma1.it/wsdeval/

[4]https://stanfordnlp.github.io/CoreNLP/

target words and have only one associated WordNet sense, that synset is chosen automatically during evaluation. Additionally, when evaluating a particular word, the WN synsets associated with it that bear different POS tags from the one indicated in the gold data are disregarded as possible options. Whenever the gold data indicates that more than one sense is a correct choice in a particular case, the system is evaluated to be correct if it selects one of them as most probable. And finally, whenever a lemma is encountered that has not been seen in the training data, the system falls back to the most-frequent-sense heuristic, using the frequency information in WordNet.

4.2 Experimental Setup

Table 1 below gives the parameters with which the neural network achieved the highest results on the evaluation data.

Parameter	Value
Embedding size	300
Word embeddings	GloVe
Lemma embeddings	WN30WN30glConOne
Bi-LSTM hidden units	2 * 200
Bi-LSTM layers	1
Dropout	20%
Dropword	0%
Optimizer	SGD
Learning rate	0.2
Initialization of LSTMs	random uniform [-1;1]
Training batch size	100
Training epochs	100K

Table 1: Parameters for the highest result obtained with the neural network.

The presence of both the GloVe vectors and the lemma embeddings in the table means that each embedding layer feeds a 300-position vector as input per word, not that the post-concatenation vector has 300 positions (that is, the final input has a dimensionality of 600). Changing the size of the LSTMs below or above 200 units has negative results on accuracy, as does adding more than one Bi-LSTM layer. Dropout is typically set to 50%, but in this case a setting of 20% produced the best results in the explored range of [0:50]. Dropword, at least the way it is applied here, does not seem to improve the results, although more experimental work is needed in order to try out a wider range of values. It remains on the agenda to test more sophisticated optimization algorithms than Stochastic Gradient Descent, as well as to integrate a learning rate decay, momentum and additional regularization techniques.

With regards to the solution outlined at the end of subsection 3.3, the parameters of the network are mostly the same. The only difference is that just one embedding layer of size 300 is used (since only the lemma embeddings are utilized) and that the number of the Bi-LSTM hidden units is 2*400 instead of 2*200.

5 Results and Discussion

Before presenting a comparison of the experimental results with other systems, Table 2 provides some select information about how different parameters influence the accuracy of the network. The top entry gives the best score that has been obtained (with the parameters in the previous table); the second entry gives the highest accuracy score obtained without dropout regularization and the third one gives the highest score obtained without dropout and without the lemma embeddings. The effect of dropout is not very big, but the addition of the lemma embeddings turns out to provide a powerful boost.

Combination	Accuracy
Best	**70.11%**
No dropout	69.98%
No lemma embeddings	68.97%

Table 2: Comparison between the best recorded setting and two other combinations of parameters.

Table 3 puts the results of this particular work in the context of the best-scoring supervised systems tested on the same dataset. The numbers are taken from Raganato et. al. (2017)[5], which gives a comparison of several such systems trained and tested on the same datasets. The results for choosing a random and the most frequent sense (MFS) are also included (the latter is a very hard baseline to beat in general, especially when good statistics are available), as well as the best results reported there for a knowledge-based system (a specific configuration of the UKB tool called UKB-g*).

[5]Note that the IMS results provided there are higher from the previous ones in Iacobacci at. al. (2016) and Zhong and Ng (2010). Thus, the 2016 results for IMS + Word2Vec (trained on SemCor) are also included ("IMS-2016"), as well as the original results from 2010 ("IMS-2010").

System	Accuracy
IMS-s+emb	**72.2%**
Context2Vec	71.8%
This work	**70.11%**
UKB-g*	68.8%
IMS-2010	68.2%
MFS	65.6%
IMS-2016	63.4%
This work - vector similarity	**61.44%**
Random	41.93%

Table 3: Comparison of this work with other systems trained on SemCor and tested on the Senseval-2 all-words lexical task. *IMS-s+emb*, *Context2Vec*, *UKB-g** and *MFS* are reported in Raganato et. al. (2017), *Random* is the performance of the current system prior to any learning.

The results show that the neural network model presented here is not lagging too far behind some of the highest reported scores on this particular dataset. Further optimizations of the network parameters, as well as more powerful input features, could bring it to par with the state of the art. The neural network is comfortably ahead of the MFS result and it also scores higher than the best knowledge-based candidate. Especially encouraging is the observation that the lemma embeddings produced via an "artificial" corpus significantly improve the score, meaning that there is still more space for enriching the input features.

Finally, a comment regarding the proposed solution that employs a vector similarity metric (introduced at the end of subsection 3.3). The result shown here is significantly lower than that of the other systems. Nevertheless, there are reasons to think that this line of research is worth pursuing. The proposed architecture does learn meaningful information, because it fares much better than a random choice heuristic. It continues to improve its accuracy even around the end of the 100K training epochs and it achieves this result with an almost unoptimized parameter configuration and with a set of lemma/sense-embeddings that is somewhat naive (it contains no information about functional words or morphologically-coded grammatical information).

6 Conclusion and Future Work

This work has presented a supervised architecture for WSD using recurrent neural networks, tested on the all-words lexical task. The model is inspired by the very successful recent applications of LSTM cells to NLP problems. The article also explores the utility of combining word embeddings learned from a large corpus of text with lemma embeddings learned from an "artificially generated" corpus based on a knowledge resource (WordNet). A comparison with the best-scoring systems on a popular evaluation dataset shows that the neural network is well-positioned with respect to them. The fact that the addition of the lemma embeddings from the pseudo-corpus improves significantly the results, signals that they could be further boosted by exploring different feature spaces and combinations of them.

There are a number of changes and additions that could be undertaken to improve the WSD algorithm. Further parameter optimization is naturally among them, as is the evaluation of other sets of word representations and the generation of improved "artificial corpora". Another improvement that could boost accuracy scores and for which RNNs are naturally suited, is allowing the model to store a representation for the previously seen sentences, i.e. to disambiguate words using whole texts as context, rather than just separate sentences. While this would not matter in tasks such as POS tagging and syntactic parsing, it is very important with regards to WSD.

And finally, a network could be trained to jointly solve two related tasks: the WSD one and that of adapting context embeddings to word sense embeddings (as discussed in 3.3). Since the similarity task is optimizing the RNN with respect to all semantic dimensions of the embedding space, the classification pathway should be able to directly benefit from that. This provides further motivation for improvements in the generation of less naive "mixed" corpora. It also remains to be tested whether such pseudo-corpora can be successfully used as training data for the supervised WSD systems themselves (as complements to expensive corpora such as SemCor).

Acknowledgements

This research has received partial support by the grant 02/12 — *Deep Models of Semantic Knowledge (DemoSem)*, funded by the Bulgarian National Science Fund in 2017–2019. I am grateful to the anonymous reviewers for their remarks, comments, and suggestions, and to my supervisor, Kiril Simov, for his support and guidance.

References

Martín Abadi, Ashish Agarwal, Paul Barham, Eugene Brevdo, Zhifeng Chen, Craig Citro, Greg S Corrado, Andy Davis, Jeffrey Dean, Matthieu Devin, et al. 2016. Tensorflow: Large-scale machine learning on heterogeneous distributed systems. *arXiv preprint arXiv:1603.04467* .

Eneko Agirre and Aitor Soroa. 2009. Personalizing pagerank for word sense disambiguation. In *Proceedings of the 12th Conference of the European Chapter of the Association for Computational Linguistics*. Association for Computational Linguistics, pages 33–41.

Yoshua Bengio, Réjean Ducharme, Pascal Vincent, and Christian Jauvin. 2003. A neural probabilistic language model. *Journal of machine learning research* 3(Feb):1137–1155.

Xinxiong Chen, Zhiyuan Liu, and Maosong Sun. 2014. A unified model for word sense representation and disambiguation. In *EMNLP*. pages 1025–1035.

Kyunghyun Cho, Bart Van Merriënboer, Dzmitry Bahdanau, and Yoshua Bengio. 2014. On the properties of neural machine translation: Encoder-decoder approaches. *arXiv preprint arXiv:1409.1259* .

Ronan Collobert and Jason Weston. 2008. A unified architecture for natural language processing: Deep neural networks with multitask learning. In *Proceedings of the 25th international conference on Machine learning*. ACM, pages 160–167.

Josu Goikoetxea, Eneko Agirre, and Aitor Soroa. 2016. Single or multiple? combining word representations independently learned from text and wordnet. In *AAAI*. pages 2608–2614.

Josu Goikoetxea, Aitor Soroa, Eneko Agirre, and Basque Country Donostia. 2015. Random walks and neural network language models on knowledge bases. In *HLT-NAACL*. pages 1434–1439.

Alex Graves. 2012. Supervised sequence labelling. *Supervised sequence labelling with recurrent neural networks* pages 5–13.

Alex Graves and Jürgen Schmidhuber. 2005. Framewise phoneme classification with bidirectional lstm and other neural network architectures. *Neural Networks* 18(5):602–610.

Sepp Hochreiter and Jürgen Schmidhuber. 1997. Long short-term memory. *Neural computation* 9(8):1735–1780.

Zhiheng Huang, Wei Xu, and Kai Yu. 2015. Bidirectional lstm-crf models for sequence tagging. *arXiv preprint arXiv:1508.01991* .

Ignacio Iacobacci, Mohammad Taher Pilehvar, and Roberto Navigli. 2016. Embeddings for word sense disambiguation: An evaluation study. In *ACL (1)*.

Richard Johansson and Luis Nieto Pina. 2015a. Combining relational and distributional knowledge for word sense disambiguation. In *Proceedings of the 20th Nordic Conference of Computational Linguistics, NODALIDA 2015, May 11-13, 2015, Vilnius, Lithuania*. Linköping University Electronic Press, 109, pages 69–78.

Richard Johansson and Luis Nieto Pina. 2015b. Embedding a semantic network in a word space. In *HLT-NAACL*. pages 1428–1433.

Mikael Kågebäck and Hans Salomonsson. 2016. Word sense disambiguation using a bidirectional lstm. *arXiv preprint arXiv:1606.03568* .

Adam Kilgarriff. 2001. English lexical sample task description. In *The Proceedings of the Second International Workshop on Evaluating Word Sense Disambiguation Systems*. Association for Computational Linguistics, pages 17–20.

Quoc Le and Tomas Mikolov. 2014. Distributed representations of sentences and documents. In *Proceedings of the 31st International Conference on Machine Learning (ICML-14)*. pages 1188–1196.

Omer Levy and Yoav Goldberg. 2014. Dependency-based word embeddings. In *ACL (2)*. pages 302–308.

Oren Melamud, Jacob Goldberger, and Ido Dagan. 2016. context2vec: Learning generic context embedding with bidirectional lstm. In *CoNLL*. pages 51–61.

Rada Mihalcea, Timothy Chklovsky, and Adam Kilgarriff. 2004. Itri-04-09 the senseval-3 english lexical sample task. *Information Technology* 25:28.

Rada Mihalcea and Dan I. Moldovan. 2001. extended wordnet: progress report. In *in Proceedings of NAACL Workshop on WordNet and Other Lexical Resources*. pages 95–100.

Tomas Mikolov, Kai Chen, Greg Corrado, and Jeffrey Dean. 2013. Efficient estimation of word representations in vector space. *arXiv preprint arXiv:1301.3781* .

George A Miller, Martin Chodorow, Shari Landes, Claudia Leacock, and Robert G Thomas. 1994. Using a semantic concordance for sense identification. In *Proceedings of the workshop on Human Language Technology*. Association for Computational Linguistics, pages 240–243.

Roberto Navigli. 2009. "word sense disambiguation: A survey". *"ACM Computing Surveys (CSUR)"* 41(2):10.

Lawrence Page, Sergey Brin, Rajeev Motwani, and Terry Winograd. 1999. The pagerank citation ranking: Bringing order to the web. Technical report, Stanford InfoLab.

Jeffrey Pennington, Richard Socher, and Christopher D Manning. 2014. Glove: Global vectors for word representation. In *EMNLP*. volume 14, pages 1532–1543.

Alessandro Raganato, Jose Camacho-Collados, and Roberto Navigli. 2017. Word sense disambiguation: A unified evaluation framework and empirical comparison. In *Proc. of EACL*. pages 99–110.

Sascha Rothe and Hinrich Schütze. 2015. Autoextend: Extending word embeddings to embeddings for synsets and lexemes. *arXiv preprint arXiv:1507.01127* .

Kiril Simov, Petya Osenova, and Alexander Popov. 2016. Using context information for knowledge-based word sense disambiguation. In *International Conference on Artificial Intelligence: Methodology, Systems, and Applications*. Springer, pages 130–139.

Kiril Simov, Petya Osenova, and Alexander Popov. 2017. Comparison of word embeddings from different knowledge graphs. In *International Conference on Language, Data and Knowledge*. Springer, pages 213–221.

Nitish Srivastava, Geoffrey E Hinton, Alex Krizhevsky, Ilya Sutskever, and Ruslan Salakhutdinov. 2014. Dropout: a simple way to prevent neural networks from overfitting. *Journal of Machine Learning Research* 15(1):1929–1958.

Kaveh Taghipour and Hwee Tou Ng. 2015. Semi-supervised word sense disambiguation using word embeddings in general and specific domains. In *HLT-NAACL*. pages 314–323.

Joseph Turian, Lev Ratinov, and Yoshua Bengio. 2010. Word representations: a simple and general method for semi-supervised learning. In *Proceedings of the 48th annual meeting of the association for computational linguistics*. Association for Computational Linguistics, pages 384–394.

Peilu Wang, Yao Qian, Frank K Soong, Lei He, and Hai Zhao. 2015a. Part-of-speech tagging with bidirectional long short-term memory recurrent neural network. *arXiv preprint arXiv:1510.06168* .

Peilu Wang, Yao Qian, Frank K Soong, Lei He, and Hai Zhao. 2015b. A unified tagging solution: Bidirectional lstm recurrent neural network with word embedding. *arXiv preprint arXiv:1511.00215* .

Wenhui Wang and Baobao Chang. 2016. Graph-based dependency parsing with bidirectional lstm. In *ACL (1)*.

Dayu Yuan, Ryan Doherty, Julian Richardson, Colin Evans, and Eric Altendorf. 2016a. Word sense disambiguation with neural language models. *CoRR* .

Dayu Yuan, Julian Richardson, Ryan Doherty, Colin Evans, and Eric Altendorf. 2016b. Semi-supervised word sense disambiguation with neural models. *arXiv preprint arXiv:1603.07012* .

Zhi Zhong and Hwee Tou Ng. 2010. It makes sense: A wide-coverage word sense disambiguation system for free text. In *Proceedings of the ACL 2010 System Demonstrations*. Association for Computational Linguistics, pages 78–83.

Multi-Document Summarization of Persian Text Using Paragraph Vectors

Morteza Rohanian
University of Tehran
rohanian@ut.ac.ir

Abstract

A multi-document summarizer finds the key topics from multiple textual sources and organizes information around them. In this paper we propose a summarization method for Persian text using paragraph vectors that can represent textual units of arbitrary lengths. We use these vectors to calculate the semantic relatedness between documents, cluster them to a number of predetermined groups, weight them based on their distance to the centroids and the intra-cluster homogeneity and take out the key paragraphs. We compare the final summaries with the gold-standard summaries of 21 digital topics using the ROUGE evaluation metric. Experimental results show the advantages of using paragraph vectors over earlier attempts at developing similar methods for a low resource language like Persian.

1 Introduction

Multi-document summarization is the task of taking the most important points of multiple input documents and put them forward in a short, cohesive way that is easy to follow. The main goal of multi-document summarization is to provide an outcome as objective as possible that can represent all documents with emphasis on key topics. Today, automatic summarization is being used as a technology that makes huge amount of online data accessible in a time that is not practicable to produce summaries manually.

Automatic summarization has been an active field of study in recent years and there are variety of approaches that have been proposed so far. Roughly, summarization methods can be split into two classes: abstractive summarization in which the system analyses the input documents and generates summaries; and extractive summarization which is the method of selecting parts of the input documents and employing them without any changes.

Extractive summarization approaches can be based on supervised learning, using document-summary pairs as training data in order to predict textual units worthy of being in the summary. These textual units can be keywords (Hong and Nenkova, 2014), phrases and sentences (Hu and Wan, 2013). Employing cluster centroids was one of the first attempt to use an unsupervised learning method for summarization (Radev et al., 2004). Sentences are represented as weighted vectors and put in clusters by applying cosine similarity. Pretrained word vectors also have been used for extractive summarization (Kageback et al, 2014). For sentence representation the authors apply 2 different approaches of adding word vectors and unfolding recursive auto-encoder (RAE).

Our method employs paragraph vector models to compute semantic relatedness between fixed-sized textual units with variable lengths (different paragraphs) and uses K-means clustering algorithm for grouping them based on their proximity. We use the centroids of clusters as the main topics of documents and choose representative paragraphs according to their weights.

2 Related Work

Based on statistical information derived from word frequency, Luhn (1958) was first to propose an algorithm for automatic extractive summarization. Later works expanded Luhns word based approach by adding other weighted statistical or linguistic features of documents. Kupiec et al. (1995) present a supervised method that considered sentences with the title-keywords in them as

Proceedings of the Student Research Workshop associated with RANLP 2017, pages 35–40,
Varna, Bulgaria, 4-6 September 2017.
http://doi.org/10.26615/issn.1314-9156.2017_005

the most important ones.

Radev et al. (2004) use centroids of news articles clusters as the most relevant topics for extractive summarization. Bonzanini et al. (2013) use variety of distance metrics for finding representative sentences and develop an algorithm for removing unimportant sentences.

After the idea of distributed word representations was proposed, it has been applied to many natural language processing tasks and demonstrated a great deal of advantage over the traditional textual representations. Kageback et al. (2014) use continuous vector representation as a basis for measuring similarity of sentences. The authors evaluate different settings of word and phrase embeddings and similarity measures on a dataset of 51 topics with corresponding abstractive summaries. Zhang et al. (2015) having word vectors as features, employ a context window to take word order into account. Their method is developed based on the Extreme Learning Machine (ELM).

There have been a few studies for Persian text summarization. Shakeri et al. (2012) use a graph theory approach to find the most important sentences of any given document. Honarpisheh et al. (2008) present a method based on a dictionary and a word segmentation system that transforms collections of documents into a matrix and takes out the most important sentences from the most important clusters.

3 Method

In this section we present our multi-document summarization method which mainly consists of two components: our two different approaches for paragraph representation and our clustering process.

3.1 Vector Representation of Paragraphs

Word embedding is a language modeling technique in which words are represented by vectors of real numbers (Mikolov et al., 2013a). The vectors are obtained by training the neural network on the basis of a text corpus and can have different number of parameters. The parameters are used to predict neighboring words of a given word by getting updated in different context. It has been shown that the final vectors represent the semantic and syntactic relationships between words much better than any other language modeling techniques. According to Bengio et al. (2003) the word vectors are generally based on three ideas :

1- Each word in the body of an n-dimensional feature vector containing the corresponding real numbers.

2- Joint probability function for words getting represented using these vectors.

3- Feature vectors learning and probability function parameters learning happening at the same time.

For providing an extractive summary we need to somehow represent sentence and paragraph vectors. A simple way is to just add or average the word vectors to make textual units vectors bigger than words. Here, we learn vector representations from a given corpus and generate the new fixed-length, n-dimensional vectors by adding all n-dimensional word vectors of a paragraph (Mikolov et al., 2013a). When paragraphs with varying length are having vectors with same dimensions, it is possible to measure their similarities. The main problem with this method is that we ignore the word order just like traditional bag-of-words models. In recent years there have been models that in addition to words and sentences, can represent paragraphs and large documents and do not need task-specific tuning of word weightings functions. Paragraph Vector is an unsupervised framework that concatenates the textual vectors with variable lengths with several word vectors and estimate the next word in a given context. They can be basis of similarity measurment between different sentences, paragraphs and documents (Le and Mikolov, 2014).

In Paragraph Vector method, each unique paragraph is represented by a vector as a column in a matrix. Each word is represented by a vector as a column in another matrix. As shown in Figure 1, paragraph and word vectors are used to predict other words within the documents by either concatenating or averaging. The generated vectors can be applied as the features of different classification or clustering techniques like K-means.

3.2 Clustering Paragraph Vectors

For extracting the most important paragraphs, first we need to group the most similar paragraphs into K clusters and capture both the central and far out paragraphs from each cluster. Each paragraph belongs to the cluster with the nearest mean, and the most central paragraph of each cluster is the

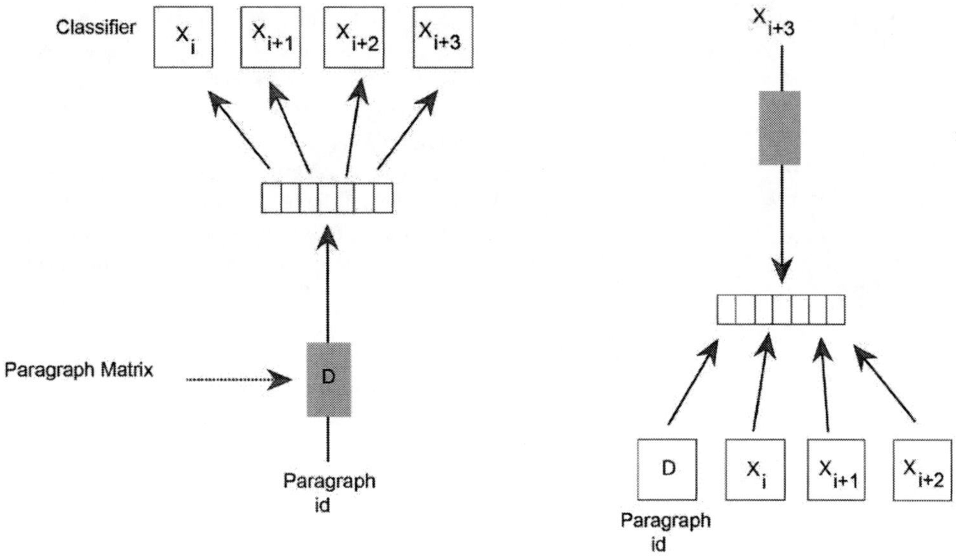

Figure 1: On the right using paragraph vectors to predict the next word of a given document and capturing word order. On the left predicting words of a paragraph using its vector.

main paragraph of that cluster. Here, we cluster close paragraphs by computing semantic similarities using specific number of latent topics within them. The most distant paragraph from the center in each cluster is the outer point of the cluster. More weight around the center of cluster shows that the central paragraph is a good representation of that cluster and we dont need to add outer paragraphs for a more balanced point of view.

To find the main paragraphs, first we initialize the K centroids randomly. Each paragraph vectors is assigned to its nearest centroid, using a specific distant metric. Each cluster center vector acts as the representation of that cluster. Then we compute the new centroids by taking the mean of all vectors assigned to each cluster. The algorithm stops until no paragraph vectors change clusters.

We use cosine similarity, which particularly used for non-zero vectors and Euclidean metric for an n-dimensional space. We weight paragraphs based on the density of each cluster. As proposed by Leskovec et al, (2014) if the ratio of the number of paragraphs divided by some power of the diameter of a cluster is below some threshold we can consider that cluster as a separated, and extract the outer point in addition to central paragraph. We use the number of dimensions of the space as the power. The number of all paragraphs in our documents divided by dimensions number power of the diameter of our vector space is our threshold. The diameter is still the maximum distance between any two points in the cluster.

3.3 Evaluation Method

For evaluation we use ROUGE (Lin, 2004), which is a recall-oriented, BLEU-like tool that considers n-gram overlaps between the automatic summaries and set of manually-provided, gold-standard summaries. There are three different ROUGE scores that are the common measurement tools used in recent publications: ROUGE-1, ROUGE-2, and ROUGE-SU4, which count matches in unigrams, bigrams, and skip-bigrams. ROUGE-1 and ROUGE-2 have the strongest association with the gold-standard summaries.

We used standard recall, precision and F-measure for reporting the relevance of summaries. Recall is the percentage of captured manually provided summaries and precision is the percentage of summaries that are in the gold-standard data. The F-measure is a weighted average of precision and recall and the outcome is bounded between 0 and 1.

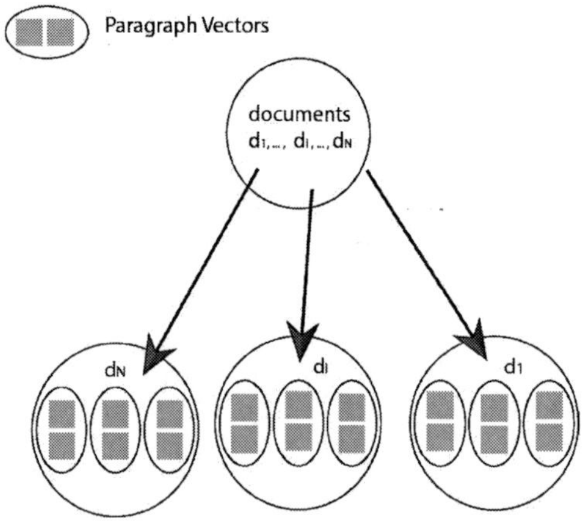

Figure 2: Clustering paragraphs into K clusters.

4 Experiments

4.1 Dataset

In order to evaluate our method we provide a dataset of 21 digital topics with each topic having between 50 and 150 paragraphs made by various users which were gathered from different Persian review sites. Each topic is about a specific property of a digital product (e.g. Screen of iPhone SE or Battery of Nikon D7200). The dataset includes gold-standard abstractive summaries of 3 for each topic.

4.2 Parameter Settings

The model in our experiment is trained on Persian Wikipedia dataset of 2.5 GB using fastText (Bojanowski et al., 2016). The dimension of vectors was considered 100 and 200 for words using Skip-gram neural networks model and 50 and 100 for paragraphs. Our models were trained 50 and 100 epochs. We chose 3 and 5 as the number of clusters and used two different distance metrics. We conduct our experiments on a 4.0GHz computer.

4.3 Results and Discussion

The multi-document summarization methods described in Section 3 evaluation results with different parameters are shown with varying parameters in Table 1. The results based on word vectors from the ROUGE-1, ROUGE-2, and ROUGE-SU4 scorings show that our model performs better with higher dimensions and smaller K. The model earns the maximum F-measure of 24.1 on word vectors and gains from training for a greater number of epochs. The results are stable among various ROUGE scores which means that the outputs with most correlation with human-provided summaries also are more fluent.

As can be seen from the Table, paragraph vectors reached the best performances for both three and five clusters compared to word vectors. Using cosine similarity measure improves the recall for different ROUGE scores evaluations while models using Euclidean metric have higher precision and F-measure. High recalls and F-measures are not achievable for our extractive summarization method due to our gold-standard summaries being abstractive.

Indicated by the results Paragraph Vector appears to be a better representation to use for clustering semantically related documents, likely because of word order consideration. The ROUGE-SU4 scores also show that in addition to semantics, paragraph vectors are more effective in capturing syntactic information.

Table 1 shows that capturing the outer topics by weighting paragraphs leads to a more balanced summary and a better ROUGE-SU4 score. It is more convincing for an individual user to read a summary from multiple perspectives. We do not observe significant improvements in ROUGE-1 and ROUGE-2 scores of our weighted models.

5 Conclusion

We described a method clustering main topics of several documents using paragraph vectors as the basis of semantic similarity between paragraphs of different lengths. The centroids of clusters considered as the main topic and paragraphs were weighted based on the distribution of data in each group. The paragraphs with more weight were extracted and compared to human-provided abstractive summaries.

The results suggest that weighting the paragraphs can make summaries more objective. However, the weighting can be combined by several other textual semantic features like the polarity of paragraphs. Considering corefrence resolution also makes the summaries more coherent and decrease the level of redundancy.

References

Yoshua Bengio, Rejean Ducharme, Pascal Vincent, and Christian Jauvin. 2003. A neural probabilistic language model. *Journal of Machine Learning Research*,

ROUGE-1

Model	Dimensions	Epochs	K	Similarity	Precision	Recall	F-measure
Word Vector	100	50	3	Cosine	21.3	26.3	23.5
Word Vectors_w	100	50	3	Euclidean	22	26.6	24.1
Word Vector	100	50	5	Euclidean	21.5	25.9	23.5
Word Vectors_w	100	50	5	Cosine	19.7	23.3	21.3
Word Vector	200	100	3	Cosine	20.5	24.3	22.2
Word Vectors_w	200	100	3	Euclidean	21.6	26.1	23.6
Word Vector	200	100	5	Euclidean	20.5	25.6	22.8
Paragraph Vectors	50	50	3	Cosine	23.5	28.9	25.9
Paragraph Vectors_w	50	50	3	Cosine	23.4	31.5	26.9
Paragraph Vectors	100	100	5	Euclidean	23.1	28.9	25.7
Paragraph Vectors_w	100	100	5	Euclidean	23.5	28.7	25.8
Paragraph Vectors_w	100	50	3	Cosine	22.9	31.8	26.6

ROUGE-2

Model	Dimensions	Epochs	K	Similarity	Precision	Recall	F-measure
Word Vector	100	50	3	Cosine	2.8	5.3	3.7
Word Vectors_w	100	50	3	Euclidean	3.8	5.6	4.5
Word Vector	100	50	5	Euclidean	3.2	5.2	4
Word Vectors_w	100	50	5	Cosine	3.3	6.1	4.3
Word Vector	200	100	3	Cosine	3.5	5.8	4.4
Word Vectors_w	200	100	3	Euclidean	3.2	5.9	4.1
Word Vector	200	100	5	Euclidean	3.3	5	4
Paragraph Vectors	50	50	3	Cosine	4	7.3	5.2
Paragraph Vectors_w	50	50	3	Cosine	4.3	8.2	5.6
Paragraph Vectors	100	100	5	Euclidean	4.4	7.3	5.5
Paragraph Vectors_w	100	100	5	Euclidean	4.1	7.9	5.4
Paragraph Vectors_w	100	50	3	Cosine	4.3	8.4	5.7

ROUGE-SU4

Model	Dimensions	Epochs	K	Similarity	Precision	Recall	F-measure
Word Vector	100	50	3	Cosine	6.2	9.1	7.4
Word Vectors_w	100	50	3	Euclidean	6.3	9.9	7.7
Word Vector	100	50	5	Euclidean	5.5	8.9	6.8
Word Vectors_w	100	50	5	Cosine	6.7	10.2	8.1
Word Vector	200	100	3	Cosine	6.7	8.4	7.5
Word Vectors_w	200	100	3	Euclidean	6.2	9.7	7.6
Word Vector	200	100	5	Euclidean	6.5	8.4	7.3
Paragraph Vectors	50	50	3	Cosine	7.9	10.1	8.9
Paragraph Vectors_w	50	50	3	Cosine	8	12.4	9.7
Paragraph Vectors	100	100	5	Euclidean	7.6	10.4	8.8
Paragraph Vectors_w	100	100	5	Euclidean	8	12.3	9.7
Paragraph Vectors_w	100	50	3	Cosine	8.3	12.3	9.9

Table 1: ROUGE scores of extractive summaries using paragraph and word vectors.

3:11371155.

Piotr Bojanowski, Edouard Grave, Armand Joulin, and Tomas Mikolov. 2016. Enriching word vectors with subword information. *arXiv* preprint arXiv:1607.04606.

Marco Bonzanini, Miguel Martinez-Alvarez, and Thomas Roelleke. 2013. Extractive summarization via sentence removal: Condensing relevant sentences into a short summary. *In Proceedings of the 36th International ACM SIGIR Conference on Re- search and Development in Information Retrieval*, SIGIR 13, pages 893896. ACM.

Mohamad Ali Honarpisheh, Gholamreza Ghassem-Sani, and Seyed Abolghasem Mirroshandel. 2008. A Multi-Document Multi-Lingual Automatic Summarization System. *In IJCNLP,* pages 733-738.

Kai Hong and Ani Nenkova. 2014. Improving the estimation of word importance for news multi-document summarization. *In Proceedings of EACL.*

Yue Hu and Xiaojun Wan. 2015. Ppsgen: learning-based presentation slides generation for academic papers. *IEEE transactions on knowledge and data engineering 27*, no. 4: 1085-1097.

Mikael K Łageb ack, Olof Mogren, Nina Tahmasebi, and Devdatt Dubhashi. 2014. Extractive summarization using continuous vector space models. *In CVSC at EACL*, pages 3139.

Julian Kupiec, Jan Pedersen, and Francine Chen. 1995. A trainable document summarizer. *In Proceedings of the 18th annual international ACM SIGIR conference on Research and development in information retrieval*, pages. 68-73. ACM.

Quoc Le, and Tomas Mikolov. 2014. Distributed representations of sentences and documents. *In Proceedings of the 31st International Conference on Machine Learning (ICML-14)*, pages. 1188-1196.

Chin-Yew Lin. 2004. Rouge: A package for automatic evaluation of summaries. *In Text summarization branches out: Proceedings of the ACL-04 workshop*, vol. 8.

Hans Peter Luhn. 1958. The automatic creation of literature abstracts. *IBM Journal of research and development 2*, no. 2 : 159-165.

Tomas Mikolov, Kai Chen, Greg Corrado, and Jeffrey Dean. 2013a. Efficient estimation of word representations in vector space. *ArXiv* preprint arXiv:1301.3781

Tomas Mikolov, Ilya Sutskever, Kai Chen, Greg S Corrado, and Jeff Dean. 2013b. Distributed representations of words and phrases and their compositionality. *In Advances in Neural Information Processing Systems*, pages 31113119.

Dragomir R Radev, Hongyan Jing, Magorzata Sty s, and Daniel Tam. 2004. Centroid-based summarization of multiple documents. *Information Processing and Management*, 40(6):919938

Jure Leskovec, Anand Rajaraman, and Jeffrey David Ullman. 2014. *Mining of massive datasets.* Cambridge University Press.

Hassan Shakeri, Saeedeh Gholamrezazadeh, Mohsen Amini Salehi, and Fatemeh Ghadamyari. 2012. A New Graph-Based Algorithm for Persian Text Summarization. *In Computer Science and Convergence*, pages. 21-30.

Yong Zhang, Meng Joo Er, and Rui Zhao. 2015. Multi - Document Extractive Summarization Using Window - Based Sentence Representation. *Computational Intelligence, 2015 IEEE Symposium Series on.* IEEE.

Gradient Emotional Analysis

Lilia Simeonova
Sofia University "St. Kliment Ohridski"
Lilia.valentinova.simeonova@gmail.com

Abstract

Over the past few years a lot of research has been done on sentiment analysis, however, the emotional analysis, being so subjective, is not a well examined discipline. The main focus of this proposal is to categorize a given sentence in two dimensions - sentiment and arousal. For this purpose two techniques will be combined – Machine Learning approach and Lexicon-based approach. The first dimension will give the sentiment value – positive versus negative. This will be resolved by using Naïve Bayes Classifier. The second and more interesting dimension will determine the level of arousal. This will be achieved by evaluation of given a phrase or sentence based on lexicon with affective ratings for 14 thousand English words.

1 Introduction

A lot of papers related to sentiment analysis show very good results, more than 80% accuracy. This kind of analysis determines whether the sentence is positive or negative (on some occasions neutral as well). Such information can be useful in terms of understanding the intentions of a given user.

The proposed research will try to take this knowledge one level deeper. This means that additional analysis will be made on the level of affection of a given sentence. Not only will this program be able to recognize positive or negative text, but will also determine its arousal level.

This project aims to examine the way people's reactions are interpreted by machines. Better and more detailed analysis of opinions, reviews, tweets, etc, can be applicable in all kinds of domains, such as commercial, retail, politics and psychological research.

2 Related Work

Hasan, Rundensteiner and Ago (2014) proposed in their paper "EMOTEX: Detecting Emotions in Twitter Messages" that twitter hashtags can be used to automatically extract data suitable for training purposes. They retrieve tweets related to four basic groups (shown below) and apply standard Machine Learning Algorithms on this data.

- Happy-Active
- Happy-Inactive
- Unhappy-Active
- Unhappy-Inactive

Proceedings of the Student Research Workshop associated with RANLP 2017, pages 41–45,
Varna, Bulgaria, 4-6 September 2017.
http://doi.org/10.26615/issn.1314-9156.2017_006

They receive good results, however, often people use misleading hashtags in order to express irony. This can lead to wrong assumptions.

3 Gradient Emotional Analysis

3.1 Circumplex Model of Affect

This paper was initially inspired by "The Circumplex model of affect". James Russell (1980) showed that emotions can be seen in a two-dimensional circular space. This space contains arousal dimension (presented in the vertical axis) and valence dimension (presented in the horizontal axis).

A diagram, showing this representation is provided in Figure 1.

The Circumplex model of affect can be applied in this paper as a starting point for more detailed investigation of emotions.

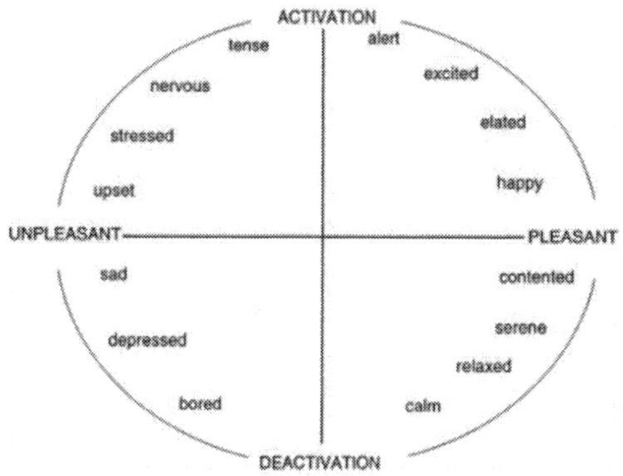

Figure 1: Circumplex model of Affect, made by James Russell.

3.2 Emotional Representation

The main idea behind the proposed paper is to analyze the input based on two different dimensions: sentiment and arousal. This is shown in Figure 2 below.

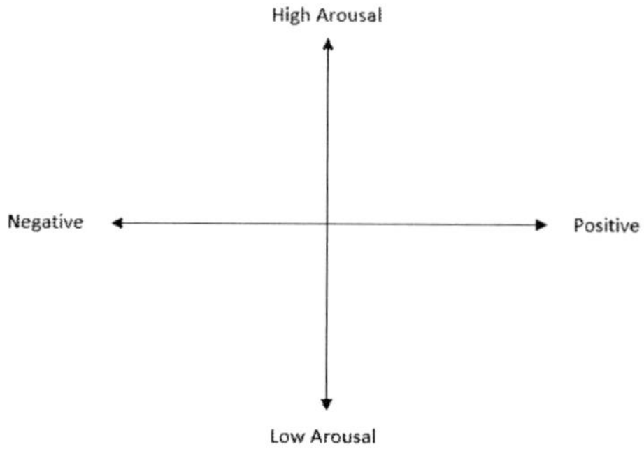

Figure 2: Emotional Analysis Diagram.

For example the verb "excite" can be categorized as positive with high arousal level, while "calm" goes under classification of positive with low arousal level.

Similar logic puts the verb "frustrate" under negative classification with high arousal, while "bore" should be negative verb with low level of arousal.

Both of the dimensions will be described in this paper.

4 Sentiment Analysis

The first part of the analysis will be achieved with the Naïve Bayes Classifier. It is one of the simplest and most commonly used Machine Learning techniques which is why it will fit perfectly in this solution.

Naïve Bayes is based on the Bayes Theorem showed on Equation 1.

$$P(A|B) = \frac{P(B|A)P(A)}{P(B)}$$

Equation 1: Bayes Theorem.

In order to create a classifier which aims to provide a positive or negative value for a given input, it needs to be decided what its features are going to be.

Feature Selection

Feature selection and extraction is a key element in the Naïve Bayes implementation. After several tests, it has been decided that a NLTK implementation of part-of-speech (POS) Stanford tagger, will be used for this experiment.

The steps performed:

- Text Preprocess – tokenization
- POS tag in tuples: (word, POS value)

After the part-of-speech tagging, only verbs, adjectives and adverbs will be extracted as they bring the most value for sentiment analysis.

5 Level of Arousal/Affect

For determining the level of Affect for a given text the Lexicon-based approach will be used.

Almost the same process is followed as the one in the Sentiment Analysis section but with one major difference.

- Text Preprocess – tokenization
- POS tag in tuples: (word, POS value)

  Exclamation mark (!) is not removed from the tokens. It can give a very good understanding of whether the person who wrote the text is feeling an emotion with high arousal.

- Retrieve the arousal value for every tagged word.
- Apply equation 2.

$$avrg\left(\sum_{arousal} Tagged\ word\right)$$

Equation 2: Formula to calculate the average arousal level of given text.

6 Experiments and Evaluation

6.1 Data

Three different datasets were used for this experiment.

A dataset with 8 885 annotated tweets has been used to train the Naïve Bayes Classifier –3 593 are labeled as positive and 5 292 are labeled as negative.

For the second part of the research – calculating the level of arousal, a lexicon with affective ratings has been used. It contains 13 915 annotated English words with a number from 1 to 9.

Another dataset has been used to verify the results from arousal level analysis. The number of tweets related with specific emotion are presented in Table 1.

Enthusiasm + Hate	700
Relief (Happiness) + Sadness	700

Table 1: Number of tweets extracted from Dataset.

6.2 Experiment and Results

Sentiment level – Naïve Bayes Classifier

10-fold cross-validation was used to measure the accuracy of the proposed algorithm. The average result from the 10 folds is 72.8%.

Arousal level

In order to verify the accuracy of the proposed arousal evaluation a training data was used with tweets annotated with words which represent active and inactive emotions. The result showed 76% accuracy for active tweets and less than 50% accuracy for inactive ones.

This means that the proposed testing approach is not working.

This failure is because the dataset which was used is automatically generated, based on hashtags. For example the following tweet extracted from the testing set is evaluated as #boredom, because the person used it with his hashtag:

"I'm so tired of being sick ALL the time!!!! #boredom".

The word "boredom" should be classified as inactive, however the language used in this tweet is showing immense frustration.

Survey

Another way of evaluating the algorithm is to ask people to evaluate manually the level of arousal.

Three people were asked to assign value 0 for inactive tweets and 1 for active.

This survey was based on 100 tweets and the average value of the results is showing 63% accuracy.

The final results are shown in Table 2.

Sentiment Analysis	72.8%
Arousal Level Analysis	63%

Table 2: Final Results.

7 Future Work

In order to improve the results in the Arousal level analysis other features need to be taken into consideration. For example, emoticons can be added in the lexicon. Another thing that might improve the results is capturing tweets written with caps lock.

8 Conclusion

This paper explores the possibilities of developing a system, which can have the capability to recognize both sentiment and arousal level of a given text. The research is using the Circumplex Model of Affect (1980) where James Russel states that the emotions can be divided in four main categories – positive- active, positive-inactive, negative-active, negative-inactive.

The implementation is based on the idea to combine two very well-known approaches – Machine Learning Approach and Lexicon Based Approach.

The first approach is to use already labeled dataset. Upon training, it can be used to classify the sentiment of an input. For its realization good results were achieved using Naïve Bayes Classifier. For future work another ML algorithm may be used.

The lexicon-based approach is used for the second part of the project. In this case the work is happening only on sentence level where the text is being tokenized. This is the moment where it is decided whether every token should be included in the analysis. An interesting part of the research was to determine which parts of the speech are best suited to be analyzed for level of affection. The idea to not exclude exclamation marks also increased the correctness of the returned values. After extracting only the needed values the arousal level is retrieved from the lexicon.

9 References

Warriner, A.B., Kuperman, V., & Brysbaert, M. (2013). *Norms of valence, arousal, and dominance for 13,915 English lemmas*. Behavior Research Methods, 45, 1191-1207

Russell J., (1980). "*A Circumplex Model of Affect*". Journal of Personality and Social Psychology. 39: 1161–1178

Mika V. Mäntylä Daniel Graziotin, Miikka Kuutila (2015) *The Evolution of Sentiment Analysis - A Review of Research Topics, Venues, and Top Cited Papers,* arXiv:1612.01556

Twitter Sentiment Analysis Training Data: http://thinknook.com/twitter-sentiment-analysis-training-corpus-dataset-2012-09-22/

Hasan M., Rundensteiner E., Agu E., (2014) *EMOTEX: Detecting Emotions in Twitter Messages,* Academy of Science and Engineering (ASE)

Liu B., Zhang L. (2013), *A survey of opinion mining and sentiment analysis,* In Mining Text Data (pp. 415-463). Springer US. DOI: 10.1007/978-1-4614-3223-4_13

Lowd D, Domingos P. (2005) - *Naive Bayes Models for Probability Estimation,* Proceeding ICML '05 Proceedings of the 22nd international conference on Machine learning Pages 529-536

Kanayama, H. and T. Nasukawa (2006) *Fully automatic lexicon expansion for domain-oriented sentiment analysis.* In Proceedings of Conference on Empirical Methods in Natural Language Processing (EMNLP- 2006)

Mohammad, S., C. Dunne., and B. Dorr. (2009) *Generating high-coverage semantic orientation lexicons from overly marked words and a Thesaurus.* In Proceedings of the Conference on Empirical Methods in Natural Language Processing (EMNLP-2009).

Qiu, L., W. Zhang., C. Hu., and K. Zhao. (2009) SELC: *A self-supervised model for sentiment classification.* In Proceedings of ACM International Conference on Information and knowledge management (CIKM-2009)

Taboada, M., J, Brooke, M. Tofiloski, K. Voll, and M. Stede (2010), *Lexicon-based methods for Sentiment analysis.* Journal Computational Linguistics archive Volume 37 Issue 2, June 2011 Pages 267-307

Pang B., Lee L., Vaithyanathan S (2002) *Thumbs up? Sentiment classification using machine learning techniques.* In Proceedings of the Conference on Empirical Methods in Natural Language Processing (EMNLP), pages 79–86, 2002.

Narayanan V., Arora I., Bhatia A. (2013) *Fast and Accurate Sentiment Classification Using an Enhanced Naive Bayes Model. In: Yin H. et al. (eds)* Intelligent Data Engineering and Automated Learning – IDEAL 2013. IDEAL 2013. Lecture Notes in Computer Science, vol 8206. Springer, Berlin, Heidelberg

Kristina Toutanova and Christopher D. Manning. 2000. *Enriching the Knowledge Sources Used in a Maximum Entropy Part-of-Speech Tagger.* In proceedings of the Joint SIGDAT Conference on empirical Methods in Natural Language Processing and Very Large Corpora (EMNLP/VLC-2000), pp. 63-70

Hernandez-Farias, DI.; Patti, V.; Rosso, P. (2016). *Irony Detection in Twitter: The Role of Affective Content.* ACM Transactions on Internet Technology. 16(3):19:1-19:24. doi: 10.1145/2930663.

Applying Deep Neural Network to Retrieve Relevant Civil Law Articles

Nga Tran Anh Hang
University of Evora / Rua Romao Ramalho 59
Evora, Portugal 7000-671 m38310@alunos.uevora.pt

Abstract

The paper aims to achieve the legal question answering information retrieval (IR) task at Competition on Legal Information Extraction/Entailment (COLIEE) 2017. Our proposal methodology for the task is to utilize deep neural network, natural language processing and word2vec. The system was evaluated using training and testing data from the competition on legal information extraction/entailment (COLIEE). Our system mainly focuses on giving relevant civil law articles for given bar exams. The corpus of legal questions is drawn from Japanese Legal Bar exam queries. We implemented a combined deep neural network with additional features NLP and word2vec to gain the corresponding civil law articles based on a given bar exam 'Yes/No' questions. This paper focuses on clustering words-with-relation in order to acquire relevant civil law articles. All evaluation processes were done on the COLIEE 2017 training and test data set. The experimental result shows a very promising result.

1 Credits

This approach was used to participate in COLIEE, an annual competition for legal Information Extraction (IE) and Retrieval. In 2017, the International Conference on Artificial Intelligence and Law (ICAIL) invited participation in a competition on legal information extraction/entailment. The COLIEE competition held 3 competitions (COLIEE 2014-2016) on legal data collection with the JURISIN workshop, and they helped establish a major experimental effort in the legal information extraction/retrieval field. We will hold the fourth competition (COLIEE-2017) in 2017 with the ICAIL conference, and the motivation for the competition is to help create a research community of practice for the capture and use of legal information. In the context of the competition on legal information extraction/entailment (COLIEE), the main approach is to build a system to address legal question answering

and relevant civil law articles.

2 Introduction

The main goal of the project is to find the relevant civil law article for a given yes/no legal question to a Japanese exam bar query. Legal Question Answering is a form of textual entailment problem. The major achievement is to capture the relationship between legal question and civil law articles. To process the system, firstly, we have to identify informative sentences/keywords from a given question by applying part of speech tagging and name entities recognition. Secondly, we retrieve related documents based on extracted sentences/keywords. Eventually, the system has to compare the semantic connection between questions and relevant sentences/keywords and make a decision as to whether they have a real relationship or not in order to give the final answer.

3 Task & Materials

Japanese civil law articles (English translation besides Japanese) will be provided, and training data consists of pairs of a query and relevant articles. The process of executing the queries over the articles and generating the experimental runs should be entirely automatic. Test data will include only queries but no relevant articles. We have 600 training corpus and 73 test corpus in total.

3.1 Information Retrieval Task

The task investigates the performance of systems that search a static set of civil law articles using previously-unseen queries. The goal of the task

Proceedings of the Student Research Workshop associated with RANLP 2017, pages 46–48,
Varna, Bulgaria, 4-6 September 2017.
http://doi.org/10.26615/issn.1314-9156.2017_007

is to return relevant articles in the collection to a query. We call an article "Relevant" to a query if the query sentence can be answered Yes/No, entailed from the meaning of the article. If combining the meanings of more than one article (e.g., "A", "B", and "C") can answer a query sentence, then all the articles ("A", "B", and "C") are considered "Relevant". If a query can be answered by both an article "D" and another article "E" independently, we also consider both of the articles

"D" and "E" to be "Relevant". This task requires the retrieval of all the articles that are relevant to answering a query.

3.2 Corpus Structure

The structure of the test corpora is derived from a general XML representation developed for use in RITEVAL, one of the tasks of the NII Testbeds and Community for Information access Research (NTCIR) project. The RITEVAL format was developed for the general sharing of information retrieval on a variety of domains.

3.2.1 Example

$< pairlabel = "Y" id = "H18-1-2" >$

$< t1 >$

(Seller's Warranty in cases of Superficialities or Other Rights)Article 566 (1)In cases where the subject matter of the sale is encumbered with for the purpose of a superficialities, an emphysematous, an easement, a right of retention or a pledge, if the buyer does not know the same and cannot achieve the purpose of the contract on account thereof, the buyer may cancel the contract. In such cases, if the contract cannot be canceled, the buyer may only demand compensation for damages. (2)The provisions of the preceding paragraph shall apply mutatis mutandis in cases where an easement that was referred to as being in existence for the benefit of immovable property that is the subject matter of a sale, does not exist, and in cases where a leasehold is registered with respect to the immovable property.(3)In the cases set forth in the preceding two paragraphs, the cancellation of the contract or claim for damages must be made within one year from the time when the buyer comes to know the facts. (Seller's Warranty in cases of Mortgage or Other Rights)Article 567(1)If the buyer loses his/her ownership of immovable property that is the object of a sale because of the exercise of an existing statutory lien or mortgage, the buyer may cancel the contract.(2)If the buyer preserves his/her ownership by incurring expenditure for costs, he/she may claim reimbursement of those costs from the seller.(3)In the cases set forth in the preceding two paragraphs, the buyer may claim compensation if he/she suffered loss.

$< /t1 >$

$< t2 >$

There is a limitation period on pursuance of warranty if there is restriction due to superficialities on the subject matter, but there is no restriction on pursuance of warranty if the seller's rights were revoked due to execution of the mortgage.

$< /t2 >$

$< /pair >$

The above is an example where query id **"H18-1-2"** is confirmed to be answerable from article numbers 566 and 567.

4 Proposed Method

4.1 Proposed Model Overview

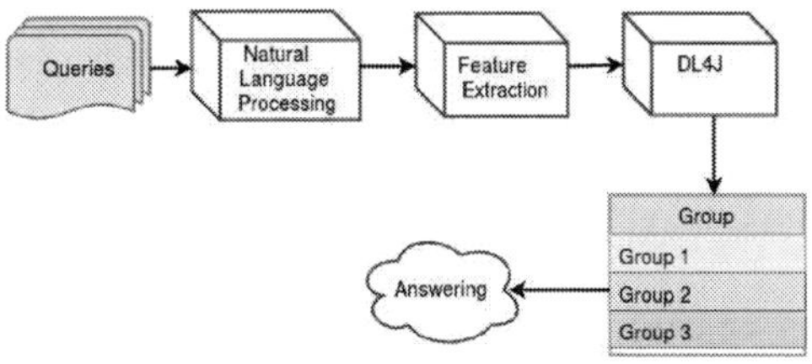

Figure 1: This is the proposed model overview

Figure 1 shows the proposed model overview. The initial idea is to try to cluster words in the training data to find the relation between them in order to retrieve relevant civil law articles.

4.2 Model Description

Each training query-article was represented as a feature vector by using Vector Representations of Words - word2vec model. These vectors were used to train neural network model - DL4J to map inputs to outputs. Deep learning is known as *universal approximator* because it can learn to approximate the function f(x) = y between any input x and any output y, assuming they are related through correlation or causation at all.

In the testing phase, given a query *q*, the model extracts its features and computes the relevance score corresponding to each article by using the

DL4J model. A higher score means the article is more relevant.

5 Result and Discussion

In our model, we focus on precision more than recall. For example, for each legal bar question the model only selects the one with the highest confidence score. Despite the fact that, there are more than one relevant document for the given question.

Noticed that one of the key properties of legal civil law articles is the reference and/or citation among documents. In other words, an article could refer to the whole of the other articles or to their paragraphs. If an article has a reference to other articles, the authors expanded it with words of referential ones. However, based on our system experiment, this approach confused the rank articles and eventually lead to a worse performance. Therefore, we ignored the reference and only took into account individual articles themselves. The results of the legal information retrieval task for data language using English is shown in the following table.

Team ID	Precision	Recall	F-measure
NOR17	0.462185	0.500000	0.480349
UA-LM	0.602564	0.427273	0.500000
Our model	0.430556	0.281818	0.340659

Table 1: COLIEE-2017 Evaluation Results

In conclusion, the main focus of our project is on precision not recall. Therefore, we approached this result. Compared to other work, this is not the best performance but the project has a very high potential and we strongly believe that, in the near future we will achieve a better approach by increasing the size of our training data, set such as utilizing dictionary of criminal law terminology, eurovoc to name a few.

Acknowledgements

I would like to express my sincere gratitude to my supervisor Prof. Paulo Quaresma for the continuous support of the project and for his patience and immense knowledge.

References

Cabrio, E., Cojan, J., Aprosio, A.P., Magnini, B., Lavelli, A. and Gandon, F., 2012. November. QAKiS: an open domain QA system based on relational patterns. In Proceedings of the 2012th International Conference on Posters & Demonstrations Track-Volume 914 (pp. 9-12). CEUR-WS. org. Vancouver.

Luisa Bentivogli, Peter Clark, Ido Dagan, Hoa Dang, and Danilo Giampiccolo, 2011. The seventh pascal recognizing textual entailment challenge, volume 9 (pp. 9-12). Proceedings of TAC.

Leif Azzopardi, Mark Girolami, and CJ Van Rijsbergen, 2008. Concept and Context in Legal Information Retrieval volume-10 (pp. 3281-3286). JURIX

Leif Azzopardi, Mark Girolami, and CJ Van Rijsbergen, 2004. Topic based language models for ad hoc information retrieval. In Neural Networks, volume-4., Proceedings 2004 IEEE International Joint Conference on IEEE

AUTHOR INDEX

Association for Computational Linguistics
209 N. Eighth Street
Stroudsburg, Pennsylvania 18360

ISBN 978-1-5108-5523-6

CURRAN ASSOCIATES INC.
proceedings.com